The
Lovebird

An Owner's Guide To

A HAPPY HEALTHY PET

Howell Book House

Howell Book House
A Simon & Schuster Macmillan Company
1633 Broadway
New York, NY 10019

Macmillan Publishing books may be purchased for business or sales promotional use. For information, please write: Special Markets Department, Macmillan Publishing USA, 1633 Broadway, New York, NY 10019.

Library of Congress Cataloging-in-Publication Data
Higdon, Pamela Leis.
The lovebird: an owner's guide to a happy, healthy pet / Pamela Leis Higdon.
p. cm.

ISBN 0-87605-430-0

1. Lovebirds.   I. Title.   II. Series.
SF473.L6H54   1997
636.6'864—dc21   97-14731
                      CIP

Manufactured in the United States of America
10 9 8 7 6 5 4 3 2 1

Series Director: Amanda Pisani
Series Assistant Director: Jennifer Liberts
Book Design: Michele Laseau
Cover Design: Iris Jeromnimon
Illustration: Laura Robbins
Photography:
  Front and back cover by Renée Stockdale
  Joan Balzarini: 14, 78
  Diane Gordon: 106
  Eric Ilasenko: 20, 21, 31
  Renée Stockdale: i, 6, 8, 13, 19, 22, 42–43, 45, 46, 50, 52, 56, 57, 61, 64, 66, 70, 71, 72, 76, 82, 87, 89, 92, 92, 100, 102, 103, 104, 110, 112, 114, 119
  Faith Uridel: 5
  B. Everett Webb: 2–3, 10, 11, 12, 15, 23, ,25, 26, 28, 29, 30, 32, 40, 44, 47, 51, 63, 68, 69, 74, 85, 98–99, 105, 108, 109, 120, 122
Production Team: Trudy Coler, Stephanie Hammett, Clint Lahnen, Stephanie Mohler, Dennis Sheehan and Terri Sheehan

Contents

Welcome
to the
World

of the

Lovebird

External Features of the Lovebird

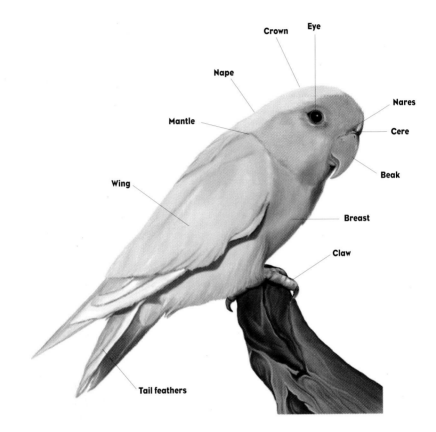

Crown

Eye

Nape

Nares

Mantle

Cere

Wing

Beak

Breast

Claw

Tail feathers

About
Lovebirds

Fascination with birds leads many of us to want to bring them into our homes as pets. Learning as much as you can about a bird's species before you buy it is the best possible course for both you and the bird. Each species, and often members of a subspecies, has a personality that may or may not mesh with you and your needs. A thorough understanding of a bird's needs, as well as your own, will help you make the wisest possible choice.

Birds do not require a daily walk or a great deal of space. Nor do they need a litter box. They do require love and companionship, understanding, a balanced diet and knowledgeable care. A treasured, properly cared for, healthy lovebird might live as long as 15 or 20

years. If you have considered carefully and have chosen the right bird for your lifestyle, every year with your lovebird can be a delight. You can wake up to her cheery chirps, share many happy moments each day and tuck her into bed with the feeling of happiness that only unconditional companionship and affection can bring.

Is a lovebird for you? The information in this book should help you decide. As you read, consider whether the needs of this charming, beautiful little parrot will fit your personality and lifestyle. A close match will help to ensure that you and a lovebird will make great companions.

A Historical Perspective

The first birds lived on earth long before humans, during the Jurassic Period, the days of the dinosaur. Occupying the air with the first birds were flying reptiles, which had begun to develop about 35 million years before. At this time, we believe that *Archeopteryx lithographica* was the first feathered, flying animal—or bird.

By studying fossils, paleontologists have learned that the first birds lived about 140 million years ago in cycad forests and were about the size of a present-day crow. Cycads are tropical and semi-tropical cone-bearing plants that are similar to palm trees. Because bird bones are lightweight or hollow to allow flight, they did not preserve well as fossils. As a result, we don't have a detailed fossil record of all the bird species that we believe may have developed between *Archeopteryx* and birds that live today.

Birds inhabited the earth during the Jurassic Period—about 140 million years ago!

Experts disagree on when parrots developed. Some accept the earliest ancestor to be *Archeopteryx verreauxi*, found in France and dating from about 30 million years ago. Others believe *Conuropsis fratercula*, found in Nebraska and dating from 20 million years ago, is the most parrot-like of ancient birds. Fossils of other parrots found in South America date from at least one million years ago.

As birds developed ways to survive, such as the ability to maneuver on the ground as well as in the air, they eventually became quite successful at finding food and claiming territories in which to live and hunt. In addition, their high rate of metabolism and warm-blooded natures gave them an edge over other animals, especially reptiles. As the number of birds increased, they competed more successfully for food, and flying reptiles eventually died out.

PARROT PARTICULARS

The lovebird shares certain traits with the Yellow-Fronted Amazon and the African Grey because they are all members of parrot species. Characteristics that all parrot species have in common include

- four toes—two pointing backward and two pointing forward

- upper beak hanging over the lower

- broad head and short neck

Today, more than 8,000 species of birds live all over the earth, although their numbers are in constant decline because of the loss of habitat and the vast numbers of wild birds captured for sale as pets. Of those, about 350 species are parrots.

What Is a Parrot?

Parrots come in all shapes and sizes. The most distinctive feature they all have is their beak. The curved upper mandible that fits neatly into the lower mandible works well to break open seeds, nuts, bones and other foods relished by parrots. The tongue is thick and used with the beak to remove foods from husks or other coverings. Parrots have distinctive feet, shared by only a few other birds, including woodpeckers. Two toes point forward and two point backward. This arrangement allows them to grip branches and other perches, as well as to walk with a waddling gait on the ground. Some parrots use their feet to grasp food as they eat. Others may stand on larger pieces of food to secure them as they eat.

Feathers grow throughout a lovebird's life—serving as enticement for a potential mate as well as camouflage.

Feathers cover all parts of a bird—from his head to the tip of his tail. Only his beak, eyes, legs and feet remain uncovered by feathers. The layer of feathers closest to the skin is called **down**. It is soft and fluffy and helps keep the bird warm. Parrots also have **powder barbs**, which are a kind of down feather. These feathers grow throughout a parrot's life and break off into bits so fine they resemble dust or powder; some species have more than others. Cockatoos, for instance, are noted for their heavy powder. This powder helps keep parrot feathers clean. The outer feathers are called **contour feathers** and include those on the wings and tail. These are the feathers you will see first; they cover the outline, or contour, of the bird and come in various colors. Current opinion on the matter is that colors serve as either good camouflage in the bird's native habitat or as a way to attract a mate.

Parrots have broad skulls and short, skinny necks. The first time you feel a parrot's neck, you may be in for a surprise. It feels like a chicken or turkey neck—thin and bony. This neck is surprisingly mobile. A parrot can move his head 180° very quickly. Like other birds, parrots have excellent eyesight, far better than that of any human.

The largest parrot in the world is the Hyacinth Macaw (about 3 feet long) from South America. The smallest is the 3-inch-long Pygmy Parrot from New Guinea. South America and Australia have many native species, Africa only a few. North America had two native species, the Carolina Parakeet and the Thick-billed Parrot. Accounts from the 1800s report clouds of these birds. Hunters killed both to extinction in the United States, although populations of Thick-billed Parrots still live in Mexico. Presently, attempts to re-introduce Thick-billed Parrots into the United States have been largely unsuccessful.

What Is a Lovebird?

A lovebird is a short, thick-bodied parrot about 5 to 6 inches long from head to tail. He has a relatively large beak for his size. The basic, or ground, color of lovebirds is green. This group of birds was named lovebirds because they groom each other constantly and sit as close together as possible when resting or sleeping.

WHERE LOVEBIRDS FIT IN

Lovebirds are classified as belonging to the order *Psittaciformes*. They are members of the family *Psittaccidae* and the genus *Agapornis*. They all come from Africa and the island of Madagascar, off Africa's east coast. Although the ground color of wild lovebirds is green, some species also have gray, pink, red, blue and yellow feathers. In addition, mutations developed by breeders come in many other hues.

In the wild, the different lovebird species live in areas that do not overlap, or overlap only by narrow margins. Birds of each of the nine species are about the same size, however, varying less than 2 inches among the different species. Their size ranges from the smallest (the 5-inch Nyasa) to the largest (the 6½-inch Black-winged). In general, all lovebirds are short bodied, with relatively large heads and short, square tails.

COLOR MUTATIONS

The word mutation appears in several sections of this book. A mutation is a change in a normal characteristic, such as color, that can occur spontaneously for no apparent reason. In the wild, a bird with a color mutation probably will not survive. Others of his species may not recognize him as one of their own

---

WHAT'S IN A NAME?

All lovebirds belong to the genus *Agapornis*. The genus name is a part of the scientific name, which will appear with more detailed discussions of each species. The scientific name is important because the common name for an animal can vary from country to country and even within a country, causing a great deal of confusion. When the scientific name is used, this confusion is avoided.

Common names are often based on a bird's coloration, who discovered or was somehow connected with the discovery of the bird or where the bird comes from in the wild. The Nyasa Lovebird, for instance, comes from Nyasaland. Dr. G.A. Fischer, who led an expedition to Lake Victoria, was the co-discoverer of the Fischer's Lovebird.

and may kill him. The color mutation may also make the bird more vulnerable to attack by predators.

The normal coloring of a species generally has developed over time to hide him in his habitat from animals of prey. A yellow, blue or white lovebird in the wild would stand out against the grasslands or the leaves of native trees, making him easy picking for a hungry predator. A predator with an outstanding mutation is also at risk. White tigers exist in captivity because they are fed by their keepers. In the wild, a white tiger could not blend in with the grasses like its normal colored relatives. Not blending in would make it impossible to hide from its prey.

Lovebirds have a beautiful and diverse array of color mutations.

In captivity, however, many mutations are prized. Breeders mate birds that show prized mutated characteristics, such as unusual color. In this way, they help develop some beautiful colors not seen in the wild, such as lutino (yellow feathers with dark eyes), white (with dark eyes), cinnamon, pied (a combination of colors in a varied pattern), blue and dark factor (darker colors than normal, such as olive green).

These mutations are appealing and they are prized by many collectors, which makes them much more expensive than normal lovebirds. A rare mutation will not make a better pet than a normal Peach-faced Lovebird, which is available all over the country at reasonable prices. The availability of normal birds also means that you are more likely to find a healthy, tame, wonderful pet bird among them than you would among the smaller numbers of rare mutations.

If you have your heart set on a mutation, however, look carefully and do your research well. Certain mutations are more prevalent in some parts of the country than in others. You may live in an area where the one you want is bred easily. If you want a blue Masked Lovebird and live in California, for instance, you should have little or no problem finding one in a pet store or from a breeder.

The Lovebird's History

Paintings and literature reveal that parrots were kept in captivity in Asian, Middle Eastern and European cultures hundreds of years ago. It is believed by many that Alexander the Great may have been among the first to bring tame parrots to Europe from Asia. The Alexandrine Parakeet (*Psittacula cyanocephala*) is named after this legendary warrior. Roman nobility kept parrots as a sign of status. Later, when European explorers began extending their searches for new and interesting treasures farther and farther abroad, they sent home many parrots, especially during the 15th and 16th centuries.

The first lovebird species were imported to Europe during the 19th century.

ARRIVAL IN EUROPE

Lovebirds were largely unknown outside of Africa until Europeans wrote of sightings. The Red-faced Lovebird (*Agapornis pullaria*) was described in detail in the early 1600s. It was the first lovebird species imported to Europe during the 19th century. Its wide distribution across the equatorial region of Africa may have made it more readily available than were other species. Other species soon followed, however. Peach-faced Lovebirds (*Agapornis roseicollis*) were acknowledged by the British Museum catalog in 1793; however, they were confused with or thought to be a variant of the somewhat similar Red-faced Lovebird. In 1817 the Peach-faced Lovebird was recognized as a separate species. They were imported to Europe from southwestern Africa for the first time in the mid-1800s.

By the beginning of the 20th century, many lovebirds had been shipped to Europe. Madagascar (Grey-headed) Lovebirds (*Agapornis cana*) were reportedly in the London Zoo during this time. Black-winged (*Agapornis taranta*) and Black-collared (*Agapornis swinderniana*) Lovebirds were both described in a book called *Shelby's Parrots* in 1836.

THE LOVEBIRD FLOURISHES

Because they are relatively easy to keep, these tiny birds thrived. Their exquisite colors and delightful ways

soon made them favorites of people all over the world. Between 1900 and 1927, four more species were discovered by European explorers: the Masked (*Agapornis personata*), Fischer's (*Agapornis fischeri*), Nyasa (*Agapornis lilianae*) and Black-cheeked (*Agapornis nigrigenis*) Lovebirds.

Today it is no longer necessary to import lovebirds from

The sweet disposition and striking colors of lovebirds contribute to their popularity.

Africa. Birds that have been hatched and hand-fed locally are available in most countries of the world. This helps to ensure a constant supply of healthy, reasonably priced pet birds. The wide choice of lovebirds bred locally gives today's birdkeepers an advantage over Europeans and Americans who had to rely on imported birds years ago: Birds bred locally are more likely to be healthy and tame.

12

chapter 2

Choosing the
Best
Lovebird

Why a Lovebird?

Perhaps you have been thinking about buying a parrot,
and perhaps you are considering a lovebird. What are
the advantages of a lovebird
over other parrot species?
There are so many.

THE PERFECT SIZE

Lovebirds are so small, compared to larger parrots, that
they need only a relatively
small cage. They take up little
space, making them ideal
both for apartments and
homes. These little birds are
hardy and suffer from few

illnesses if kept clean and fed a balanced diet. Some of the larger birds delight in tearing up phone lines, cabinets, baseboards, books and doors, in short, anything they can get their beaks on. Larger birds have stronger beaks, so anything they can grab, they can usually destroy. The lovebird's smaller size makes this an unlikely scenario.

WELL-MANNERED

Compared to the call of a macaw or a cockatoo, which cannot only be deafening, but can also upset neighbors far and near, lovebirds are relatively quiet. A lovebird will call to her owner when he or she is out of sight, but the sound will rarely carry through walls unless the windows or doors are open, and then it barely competes with the noise of wild birds.

CUTE COMPANIONS

Lovebirds have gentle dispositions and make top-notch companions.

These tiny birds come in so many beautiful colors. The first lovebirds I ever saw were about 7 weeks old. They were so charming, I wanted to scoop them up and take them all home. Why do we want pets? We want them for the affection they provide and the way they make us feel needed. Lovebirds are flock birds and they need

companionship, but not necessarily another bird. If you buy a single bird, he will rely on you for attention. You will become the flock for this sociable little creature.

Lovebirds would make bad poker players. Not only do they not hide their feelings well, they don't hide them at all. This expressiveness makes them a joy to be with and to watch. To be the object of a lovebird's affection will give you an amazing amount of satisfaction and happiness. It is impossible to be anything but cheerful as you watch this tiny treasure express his curiosity about his surroundings.

Is a Lovebird Right for You?

When choosing a bird, you should consider many factors:

- Noise level is always at the top of my list. Whether you live in an apartment or a detached home, this will be important.

  Lovebirds chatter and call to one another and to their human companions using a high-pitched sound. Many agree that the most annoying call belongs to the Peach-faced Lovebird. Fischer's Lovebirds, though not loud, have a piercing, shrill whistle and a high-pitched twittering. When it comes to assessing noise level, though, you must decide for yourself. If you are unsure about the potential noise level of these birds, visit a breeder or pet store and observe the lovebirds at several times of the day for extended periods.

Keep in mind that gregarious lovebirds tend to chatter to each other.

- Parrots come in many sizes, from the tiniest 5-inch-long lovebirds and parrotlets to the largest 3-foot-long Hyacinth Macaws (*Anodorhynchus hyacinthinus*). Size is an important issue to consider. The larger the bird, the louder the noise and the more difficult to house properly. The small size of the lovebird makes her an ideal apartment or home dweller. Caging is relatively inexpensive and easy to find.

- Cost is another important consideration when buying a bird. Because lovebirds have been bred successfully in the United States for many years, hand-fed popular species should be readily available at a reasonable cost. Mutations may be more expensive, however, especially those of unusual color.

- When some people buy a parrot, speaking ability is a concern. It is never a good idea to buy a bird for talking potential. Even members of other parrot species more likely to talk, such as the African Grey or Yellow-headed Amazon, are not all guaranteed talkers. Most experts agree, though, lovebirds do not talk.

- When considering a lovebird, remember that in the wild they are small creatures in a dangerous world. Those small animals that survive are often bold and aggressive. Lovebirds will attack and kill other species, including much larger birds. Adding them to a group of birds of a different species can mean trouble and should be avoided.

Where to Find the Lovebird for You

By now you, too, are charmed by lovebirds, but you wonder just how to choose one. First, consider species. Unless you are extremely fortunate, you will mainly find three lovebird species available at reasonable prices: the Peach-faced Lovebird, the Masked Lovebird and the Fischer's Lovebird. These species are most available because they are easy to breed in captivity. Among these three species, there are numerous mutations for those who want a more exotic-looking bird. Keep in mind, though, that more unconventional birds are also more expensive. An exotic color will not make a bird a better pet, and in my opinion the natural colors of lovebirds are wonderful.

You've studied the personality traits of these species and you are wondering which will be most suited to you. Lovebirds, like people and all other animals, have their own personalities. Although general things can be said about birds of a species, each bird is different. Once you have decided to buy a lovebird, avoid buying one on impulse. One of the secrets to buying the perfect bird is doing research. The perfect bird will come from a clean establishment, whether that is a pet store, a hobby breeder or a professional breeder. Visit as many of these sources as you can find in your area. Take the time to study a group of birds and handle them; you will soon find the one with the personality for you. Do you want a cuddler? An independent bird? An energetic entertainer? List the qualities you want in an ideal lovebird and don't give up until you find a bird that has them all.

> ### IS THIS LOVEBIRD HEALTHY?
>
> Here are some of the signs of a healthy lovebird. Look for these when selecting your pet.
>
> lively, shiny eyes
>
> smooth feathers
>
> a hearty appetite
>
> an energetic, outgoing personality
>
> a clean cere (the area above the bird's beak that covers his nostrils)
>
> clean legs and vent
>
> an upright posture
>
> a full-chested appearance

BIRD SHOWS

One of the best ways to see as many lovebirds as possible in a short time is to attend a bird show. Show dates are listed in several pet magazines. Bird show judges must have raised and shown the kind of bird they judge. These people are interested in lovebirds and are always happy to share their interest and knowledge. Approach them after a show, however. During a show they are extremely busy. Be sure to tell the judge that you are interested in a pet and explain which qualities you would like in a lovebird as well as the species you think you are interested in.

PET STORES AND BREEDERS

Pet stores are the logical first place to look. Take notes about the kinds of birds you find, the prices and the condition of the stores. Also note the helpfulness and knowledge of store personnel. Next, check breeders. Both stores and breeders should be held to the same standards of cleanliness.

- Are the cages kept clean? Keep in mind that birds will pass droppings about every twenty minutes. When you multiply that by the number of birds in the cage, you can see how the droppings will quickly add up. Nevertheless, the cage bottom should be changed at least once a day. How clean are the perches? They should be free of droppings.

- Food and water containers must be spotless and should always be located away from the birds' perching spots to prevent contamination from droppings. Water must be kept clean, preferably without the addition of liquid vitamins or other supplements, which can spoil during the day. (Supplements often give the water a yellowish, oily appearance.)

- How many birds are kept in a cage? If there are too many, the birds will appear to be crowded and uncomfortable. The cage may be overly dirty and the food soiled. The birds will exhibit their unhappiness by attacking each other. Are the birds ever taken out for exercise and socialization?

- What kind of diet are the birds fed? A balanced diet of seeds, fruits and vegetables will help ensure healthier birds than those that are fed only seed. Is the fresh food (fruits and vegetables) fresh looking? It should not be allowed to remain in the cage long enough to spoil. Experienced birdkeepers remove fresh food after only a few hours. If it looks wilted, it should not be in the cage. Is the store or breeder's establishment clean in general? Where is food kept? Is it of high quality?

BIRD CLUBS

For more backup, check with bird clubs in your area. Attend a few meetings and ask for recommendations on pet stores and breeders. People who belong to these clubs are friendly, interested in lovebirds and anxious to share information with others. This is a vital source of information, and it will cost you only the nominal dues if you decide to join. You may also make some interesting friends.

Choosing the Right Lovebird

One important consideration should be age. Young birds are easier to tame than older birds. Ideally, the best bird is one that was hand-fed: A person fed the baby instead of her parents. This method causes the bird to become used to humans and to learn to trust them. A hand-fed bird will bond to you as she did to her feeder. That doesn't mean you will not have to work with your bird to achieve a great relationship. It means that you and your bird will have a much easier time establishing your connection.

HAND-FEEDING

You will want a bird that is between 6 and 8 weeks old—weaned from hand-feeding formula. If he is not already weaned and eating regular food, that will become your job. Although some people want to do this and some also want to take over the hand-feeding of their new baby lovebird, I do not recommend it.

A hand-fed bird bonds easily since she has already learned to trust humans.

Even for experienced bird-keepers, hand-feeding and weaning are time-consuming, anxiety-inducing pastimes. I keep some birds that I hand-fed and weaned and some birds that were hand-fed by others; I can assure you that the bonding (and love I feel) between me and my birds was no different for those birds hand-fed by others. It was certainly less stressful to let others do it for me.

In addition to being more trustful, hand-fed birds are less noisy than parent-raised birds. Perhaps best of all, many of them like to cuddle. As small as he is, a lovebird may look like a creature you can easily bend to your will. It's best to keep in mind that a hand-fed love-bird will cuddle and he will play—but he will do so when he feels like it, not when you think the time has arrived. This is true parrot behavior.

In a perfect world, hand-feeding means that someone took the time to feed each chick clean, warm, nutritious formula either with a spoon or a syringe every two hours, then every three hours and so on twenty-four hours a day. This goes on until the chick is ready to be introduced to and convinced to eat the diet of an adult bird. As this ideal hand-feeder feeds the bird, she or he will talk lovingly to the bird and stroke her to help her get used to humans. Unfortunately, not all hand-feeders are committed to the well-being of the bird and will not handle her regularly, but will feed in a more assembly-line style. This results in a bird that is as untrusting of humans as a wild-caught bird.

The ideal time to get your lovebird is when he is between 6 and 8 weeks old.

How can you tell the difference? When you have chosen a bird, ask to hold her on your hand or finger. If she shies away from you in fright, she was probably not hand-fed properly and it will take extensive training to accustom her to humans. If she seems confident enough to step onto your finger or shoulder, she was hand-fed as she ought to have been. You can tame a hand-shy bird, but be prepared for a large commitment of time and patience.

SIGNS OF GOOD HEALTH

Once you have the bird out of the cage, run your finger gently down his **chest**. Baby birds are nice and plump. They grow and gain weight quickly, soon outweighing their parents. They must put on the extra fat necessary for weaning. The chest should feel firm and full; the keel bone down the center of the chest should not feel sharp or stand out, which would indicate an underweight, or perhaps sick, bird.

Look carefully at the bird's **feathers**. He should have no bald spots. Some birds pull out their feathers; this is a sign of frustration and unhappiness that can become a hard-to-break habit. His feathers should be clean and smooth. Both wings should hang evenly. The bird's grip on your fingers should be firm and he should have all of his toes intact. His breathing should be slow and even.

If you have chosen an eye-ringed species, the **eye ring** should be smooth and white, not puffy or discolored. How can you know for sure that a bird is young? The best way is to look at the **beak**. Lovebird chicks have black beaks. As they mature, the lighter colored beaks grow in. When they are of weaning age, though, they should still have some black left on their beaks.

This olive baby lovebird still has black left on her beak. This will change to a lighter color as she matures.

Stand back and look at all of the birds in the cage. It's time to find a healthy bird. Healthy birds have clear, bright **eyes**. Their **nostrils** are clear and their beaks are of normal length and have clean, sharp edges. Feathers are in good condition. Those under the bird's tail (called the **vent**) should be clean and unstained. Diarrhea causes stains on the vent feathers. Normal droppings will not stain the vent feathers. A healthy bird will be free of cuts and abrasions. She will sleep with one foot up, balancing on the other foot.

UNDER THE WEATHER

A sick bird will be inactive for long periods of time. may sit on the floor of the cage if she is terribly ill. Sick birds are often fluffed to keep warm and sit on both feet. Fluffed birds look appealing, but should be avoided at all costs. Sick birds may have runny, dull-looking eyes and/or clogged nostrils. Their breathing may be wheezy and labored if they have respiratory problems. If there are a lot of sick birds in a cage, avoid buying a bird from that group.

Birds do not exhibit obvious signs of illness until they are extremely ill. This serves them well in the wild, where predators single out sick animals as easy targets or their own species drives them out of the flock because of the danger they present by attracting predators. It is only when they are too ill to be able to put forth the energy to disguise their state of health that they become obviously sick. If a bird is that sick, do not buy her. She probably cannot be saved.

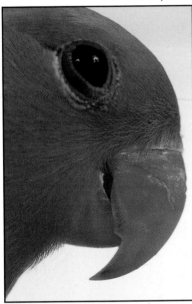

A healthy lovebird has a sharp beak, bright eyes and clear nostrils.

This may seem like a tremendous amount of information to take in and use to evaluate a bird. As you look at birds, though, you will begin to pick out the sick birds from the well, the hand-fed and tame from those still untamed. It will be easier if you can remember to look at the cage and the food, then the bird from head to toe. There will be fewer sick birds than well ones; they should stand out by comparison. The more you look, the easier it will become, particularly if you compare the photos of healthy birds in this book to the birds you see.

A Secondhand Bird?

Sometimes people buy birds and find that they cannot keep them, for various reasons. Perhaps a friend or neighbor has noticed your interest in his or her bird and has asked if you would like to adopt him. If the bird is healthy and tame, why not? In such transactions, the bird usually comes with a cage, toys, dishes and other accessories. I know of many instances in which the bird is much happier with his new owner, particularly if his former owners had not been able to offer him the love, time, security and nutrition he needs.

One Bird or Two?

The temptation for first-time lovebird owners is to buy two. The name seems to indicate that they need a companion to be happy. It's true that a lovebird needs a companion, but it need not be a bird. In fact, if you buy two birds, they will bond to each other and seek their needed companionship from each other—even if they were hand-fed. They will tolerate you and may even interact with you, but the bond will not be as strong as it would have been had you bought only one bird.

On the other hand, if you buy only one bird, you will need to offer her the attention another bird would have given her. This doesn't mean twenty-four-hour-a-day tending; it means you will have to pay a reason-able amount of attention to the bird. She will need lots of playtime out of the cage and with you. You will find that she wants to cuddle and chirp at you—I can certainly think of a lot of less enjoyable activities.

Two lovebirds are more likely to bond with each other than to look for attention from their owner.

It does take planning at first, though, to make playing with your bird a habit. If you cannot offer this kind of interaction, your bird may become emotionally dam-aged. Flock animals eat, sleep and play together. You will find that your bird will want to play with you and will eat best if you eat at the same time. He may even want to share your food with you. Not only is this a good "flock" activity, it is a good time to bond—and it is fun.

So, one bird or two? The choice is yours and should be made before you make your purchase, depending on how much time you can devote to your bird and how close you want the relationship to be. If you are in doubt, buy one bird. If you find that you cannot give him enough attention, buy a second bird. Sometimes, though, people buy two birds, and then find that the birds will not bond to them, but snuggle contentedly with each other. If you decide to buy two birds, choose another of the same species as your first bird. Mixing species could result in the death or injury of one of the birds.

BUYING A SECOND BIRD

If you decide to buy a second bird after you have established one bird, proceed with caution. Don't let the name lovebird fool you. These little beauties are territorial. Think of a 2-year-old child shouting "Mine!" about everything and backing it up by hitting and biting. Lovebirds are not only territorial, they are aggressive and tough about anything they perceive to be a threat to what they perceive as theirs.

No matter where you buy the new bird, he may carry a disease home to your old bird. Quarantine any new bird in a separate room for ninety days, observing him carefully for signs of illness. Do not buy a bird with any symptom that signals illness.

chapter 3

All Kinds
of Lovebirds

Classifying Lovebirds

There are several ways to classify lovebirds. Some experts sort them into groups of those that are sexually dimorphic (males and females look significantly different, especially in color) and those that are not. Species in which the males are visually different from females include Madagascar Lovebirds (*Agapornis cana*), Red-faced Lovebirds (*Agapornis pullaria*) and Black-winged Lovebirds (*Agapornis taranta*).

Another grouping centers on those that have an eye ring of bare, white skin and those that do not. Eye-ringed species include the Masked (*Agapornis personata*), Fischer's (*Agapornis fischeri*), Nyasa (*Agapornis lilianae*) and Black-cheeked (*Agapornis nigrigenis*) Lovebirds.

Those that do not have an eye ring are the Madagascar (*Agapornis cana*), the Red-faced (*Agapornis pullaria*) and the Black-winged (*Agapornis taranta*) Lovebird. These three lovebirds are sexually dimorphic.

In between those two groups is the Peach-faced Lovebird (*Agapornis roseicollis*), which does not have an eye ring and is not sexually dimorphic. One lovebird that falls into neither group is the Black-collared (*Agapornis swinderniana*) Lovebird. It has an inconspicuous feathered eye ring. This species is not sexually dimorphic.

The Peach-faced Lovebird

One of the most popular and available lovebirds is *Agapornis roseicollis*, commonly called the Peach-faced Lovebird. These beautiful birds breed easily in captivity and have made themselves favorites of many pet owners. Understanding how a bird lives and behaves in the wild is important to a pet owner; it is one of the best ways to understand the behavior and needs of your pet.

Normal Peach-faced Lovebird.

BEHAVIOR IN THE WILD

In the wild, Peach-faced Lovebirds are plentiful and live in small flocks. Their territory extends over a large area of the southwest coast of Africa, including Angola,

Botswana and Zambia. These birds inhabit dry scrublands that range from the lowlands up to about 5,300 feet, where they are usually seen near water holes. During harvest seasons when seed crops are abundant, they can be seen feeding in flocks consisting of hundreds of birds.

Origins

Although this bird was discovered by Europeans and recognized in the catalog of the British Museum in 1793, it was not acknowledged by the British as a separate species until 1817. After the mid-1800s, Peach-faced Lovebirds were imported to Europe in great numbers. Because they bred readily and were relatively easy to keep, they became favorites of European hobbyists. World War I and World War II caused the deaths of many of these birds. European and American breeders worked hard to rebuild stocks.

Special Characteristics

Peach-faced Lovebirds enjoy flying and are fun to watch. They specialize in straight, fast flight, interspersed with regular glides. During the gliding phases and while on the ground hunting seeds or berries, Peach-faced Lovebirds call to each other. Pet Peach-faced Lovebirds call to each other and to their owners in the same way. Wild females are particularly interesting when they are nesting. They nip off small twigs or strips of bark from trees. A female will tuck these bits of nesting materials into her rump, back and upper tail covert feathers. If a piece is more than a few inches long, she may bend it before tucking it in with the rest. Usually, she will gather about six pieces and stuff them into her feathers with both ends of each piece showing.

This information is not only interesting, it is useful; a pet female Peach-faced Lovebird may gather toothpicks or pieces of paper around the house, tuck them into her feathers and fly back to her cage, where she may attempt to build a nest. Even unmated females will do this; it is instinctive behavior, something she will do without being taught. She may also carry paper or other material in her beak.

COLOR VARIATIONS

The term "wild-colored" refers to the color closest to that of wild birds of a species. Wild-colored Peach-faced Lovebirds have a peach, or salmon, colored face, neck and throat. (The scientific name means rosy-headed lovebird.) Their wings and bodies are a light green and the upper tail coverts and rumps are a stunning cobalt blue. Their flight feathers are black. Their beaks are horn colored, their eyes brown and their legs gray. Males and females are so similar it would be difficult for anyone but an expert to tell them apart. Peach-faced Lovebirds are about 6 inches long, from the tops of their heads to the tips of their tails.

Creamino Peach-faced Lovebird.

Mutations of the Peach-faced Lovebird have produced many beautiful colors, which also add to the bird's popularity. There are more mutations of this species available than among any other lovebird. Mutation colors include a blue-green (also called pastel blue, sea-green, Dutch blue and par blue), yellow, lutino (the ground color is yellow but the face is still a peach color and eyes are normal), pied (a mottled yellow and green), cinnamon, white-faced, orange-faced, dark factor (this causes ground color feathers to be darker green than normal—an olive green) and various combinations. Occasionally silver, golden cherry-head, violet and mustard can be found.

Because they are so readily available, hardy and reasonably priced, Peach-faced Lovebirds are an excellent first bird. Peach-faced Lovebirds are also called Rosy-faced Lovebirds and Rose-headed Lovebirds. Keep in mind that this is the most aggressive of the lovebird species. They have been known to attack each other as well as much larger birds. Peach-faced Lovebirds are not suitable for housing with other birds. This aggression is based on an instinctive need to protect their territory. If you understand that these birds have this trait, you can adjust your circumstances to make this your only bird or have only a male and a female Peach-faced Lovebird.

The Fischer's Lovebird

Fischer's Lovebirds (*Agapornis fischeri*) are also popular pets and are readily available through pet stores, breeders and hobbyists.

Normal Fischer's Lovebirds.

ORIGINS

Although discovered in 1887, Fischer's Lovebirds were not imported into Europe until about 1926. The first European sighting of this lovebird was made by Dr. G.A. Fischer, who was exploring the area around Lake Victoria. One bird was brought to Cleveland, Ohio, by Mr. K.V. Painter in 1925.

Fischer's Lovebirds proved easy to breed and often began nesting soon after they had arrived in a new country. Records indicate that they were bred successfully in several countries, including Germany, in the late 1920s. By 1931, The Berlin Zoo had reared sixty-eight Fischer's Lovebirds. Because they were established quickly and imported in large numbers, they soon became popular pet parrots.

IN THEIR NATIVE HABITAT

The wild habitat of Fischer's Lovebirds includes only a small area to the south of Lake Victoria on the grassy plains of Tanzania where acacia, palm and baobob trees grow. Wild Fischer's Lovebirds prefer to live in these trees, especially those that grow in small clusters on the plains.

These birds eat acacia and grass seeds, as well as millet. They chirp to each other as they fly quickly in

straight lines from point to point. Females carry twigs, bark and other nesting materials in their beaks. A pet may find and carry small strips of paper back to her cage. Females like to dip nesting material in water, which some believe is to soften it.

These birds are often killed in their native habitat because they destroy the grain crops they favor. They generally live in small flocks in the wild. A wild-colored Fischer's has a dark orange head and chest, with a green body and wings. The back of the head is olive

Yellow Fischer's split to Lutino.

green. The neck collar is yellowish orange. The feathers on the bird's underparts are yellowish green. It has a distinctive white eye ring around a brown eye. The beak is reddish orange and the legs are gray.

The rump is blue. These birds are not sexually dimorphic; you cannot tell males and females apart by looking at them.

CHARACTERISTICS

This bird has a shrill call. Twittering is high-pitched. Adult Fischer's Lovebirds are about 5½ to 6 inches long. Breeders have developed several mutations of the Fischer's Lovebird, including blue, pastel blue, yellow, greenish yellow, yellow-green pied, cinnamon or white (or albino). Cinnamon and pastel blue are rare. Mutations can be quite expensive.

Fischer's Lovebirds are considered an excellent bird for the first-time owner because they are robust and easy to handle. These birds have a lot of energy and are fun to watch in their acrobatic play.

The Masked Lovebird

Masked Lovebirds (*Agapornis personata*) are another readily available species. Although the first sighting is not well-documented, they were imported to North America and then to Europe in the early 1900s. They were reportedly first bred in the United States by Mr. K.V. Painter of Cleveland, Ohio, in 1926 and were imported into the United States in large numbers in 1927. By 1928, they had been bred successfully in Switzerland, and German breeders were successful with this bird by about 1930.

Black-masked Lovebird.

TANZANIAN NATIVES

Masked Lovebirds are native to part of the Great Rift Valley in northeast Tanzania, where they prefer to perch in baobob, palm and acacia trees. Like the Fischer's Lovebird, these birds feed on a variety of grass seeds,

31

acacia seeds and millet. Because they are destructive to seed crops, these birds are often killed in their natural habitat. Groups were also introduced to Dar es Salaam in Tanzania and in Nairobi, Kenya, where they thrive.

CHARACTERISTICS

Females carry nesting material consisting of twigs and bark in their beaks. The brownish-black head of the Masked Lovebird contrasts dramatically with its yellow chest and neck. The rest of the feathers are green. The beak is red and the legs are gray. The white eye ring is pronounced. It would be difficult for anyone but an expert to tell males from females.

Blue Masked Lovebird.

Masked Lovebirds are about 5½ inches long from the top of the head to the tip of the tail. Available mutations include a blue Masked Lovebird; the normally green feathers are a lovely greenish blue and the normally yellow feathers on the chest and throat are white. The head remains brownish black but the beak is horn colored. Other mutations include yellow, pied, cinnamon, cobalt blue, mauve and dark-eyed white. These mutations are unusual and may be expensive and difficult to find.

Masked Lovebirds are considered good first birds because they are vigorous and readily available. Because this lovebird is aggressive, it is best to buy one that was hand-fed as a chick. This will help ensure that she will relate well to her owner. Hand-fed Masked Lovebirds are tame, lovable pets. Other common names for this bird include the Black-masked Lovebird and the Yellow-collared Lovebird.

The Nyasa Lovebird

The Nyasa Lovebird (*Agapornis lilianae*) was first encountered by European explorers in 1864, but it was not named until 1894. Its common name is derived from its homeland, formerly called Nyasaland, which now comprises parts of Malawi, Tanzania, Mozambique and eastern Zambia. In addition, some have been reported in Zimbabwe.

ORIGINS

They are reported to be particularly concentrated in part of lowland areas of the Zambesi Valley near Victoria Falls. The scientific name was given to the bird in honor of Lilian Sclater, the beautiful sister of a famous ornithologist of the time. The first Nyasa Lovebirds arrived in Europe in 1926—probably in Germany, although they quickly spread to France. In 1927, the German magazine *Vögel ferner Länder* (*Birds of Foreign Lands*) noted that a hand-fed Nyasa Lovebird had been taught to say "Na Komm, wo bist Du denn?" ("Come on, where are you then?"). This is one of the few reports of a lovebird learning to talk.

Although they bred easily there as well as in the United States and Australia, they are now difficult to find in the United States and are expensive.

CHARACTERISTICS

For about thirty years, the Nyasa was thought to be the same species as the Peach-faced Lovebird. When you see pictures of this appealing little bird, it becomes obvious why. As you look more closely, however, you can see the differences easily: The Nyasa Lovebird has a white ring of featherless skin around its eyes, and the Peach-faced Lovebird does not.

This is the smallest of the eye-ringed species. (It weighs about 1½ ounces and is about 5 inches from head to tail.) The Nyasa Lovebird has a red beak and the Peach-faced Lovebird has a horn-colored beak. The Nyasa Lovebird is also confused by some with the Fischer's Lovebird, but the Nyasa has green rump feathers while the Fischer's are blue.

LIFE IN THE WILD

In the wild, these birds live mainly in mopane wood-lands, but also inhabit acacia trees on the Zambesi Valley floodplain. They feed on the ground and the tops of trees and can often be seen at water holes or lakes, drinking or bathing. This tells us several things—they need to be offered water to bathe in fre-quently and should have a constant supply of clean drinking water. Some experts believe this lovebird is especially sensitive to chlorinated water or hard tap water that has a variety of chemicals in it. They recom-mend boiled water for these birds. The bird's behavior in the wild also tells us that, in contrast to many other species, if these birds fly to the floor of their cages to eat, it is not an indication of poor health.

Wild birds eat a combination of seeds, grains, berries and other fruit and plant buds. Their flight is beauti-ful: swift and direct. The call of wild Nyasa Love-birds has been compared to a shrill clatter of chains rattling together. Wild Nyasa females carry nesting material in their beaks. These lovebirds seem to nest all year in the wild, so it's best not to offer a pet fe-male a nest box because she may become obsessed with nesting.

Males and females are similar; only an expert could tell them apart. The Nyasa Lovebird is not aggressive and is more accepting of other lovebirds than any other lovebird species. One of its appealing features is that Nyasa Lovebirds (generally) accept birds of other species, such as budgies and cockatiels. Another plus is the relatively low noise level—especially after the bird gets used to his surroundings.

Mutations are few, probably because these birds are so difficult to come by. There is a lutino mutation, which is a yellow bird with a pinkish face and throat, red beak, white flight feathers and black eyes. Some report a blue mutation. Other common names for the Nyasa Lovebird are Nyasaland Lovebird, Lilian's Lovebird and Strawberry-headed Lovebird.

The Madagascar Lovebird

The Madagascar Lovebird (*Agapornis cana*) is native to the island of Madagascar, off the east coast of Africa. Perhaps because of its relatively isolated habitat, it did not come to the attention of many European or American lovebird collectors until after World War II. It was first brought to Europe during the later 1800s, but import/export bans prevented them from widespread distribution in either Europe or the United States.

HOMELAND

In their homeland, they live in open scrubland or desert brushland along the coast or at the base of mountains, below 3,000 feet. Although they can be seen perching in trees at the edges of the scrubland or on telephone lines, they do not live in the forests. They feed on berries, grains, grass seeds and on rice that villagers have put out to dry. Because they destroy grain and seed crops, natives seek them out and kill them.

CHARACTERISTICS

Their call is high-pitched and shrill. In the wild, the flight of the Madagascar Lovebird has been described as fast and twisting. If frightened, they screech as they fly up and away. The female Madagascar Lovebird is one of those that carries nesting materials in her rump feathers. This is important for pet owners to know because they may see their bird pick up and carry small pieces of paper in her feathers and wonder why. This is instinctive behavior; it does not need to be taught. She will do it, guided strictly by inborn signals.

In general, these birds are shy, especially compared to their more aggressive relatives, the Peach-faced Lovebirds. They are not without spunk, however, and have been known to bite hard enough to draw blood if they feel threatened. Hand-fed birds relate well to humans and will be less inclined to bite than will those that were parent raised. It is always a good idea, though, to avoid backing any bird into a corner or trying to handle him if he is frightened. Biting is their only real defense. Females may be a bit more temperamental than males; in the wild, females must be somewhat aggressive to protect their nests and their young.

Hand-fed or tame Madagascar Lovebirds are quite sweet to their owners. This is one of the smaller lovebird species, at 5 inches from head to tail; the bird also has a more slender body than other lovebirds. The Madagascar Lovebird species has no eye ring and is sexually dimorphic—that is, you can tell males from females by looking at them. A male has a light gray head, throat and chest. The rest of the male's feathers are green, with black feathers under the wings. His eyes are dark brown, and his beak, legs and feet are gray. A female Madagascar Lovebird is all green, with her head, throat and chest a yellowish green. Her eyes are brown; her beak, legs and feet are gray. Their beaks are the smallest of all lovebird species.

For those of us who appreciate subtle beauty, the Madagascar Lovebird is the loveliest of them all. There are no known mutations of the Madagascar Lovebird. Common names include Grey-headed Lovebird and Lavender-headed Lovebird. Although these birds may be difficult to find, a diligent effort may help you locate one.

The Black-winged Lovebird

The Black-winged Lovebird (*Agapornis taranta*) is the largest of the lovebirds. It averages almost 7 inches from head to tail and weighs close to 2 ounces. Hand-fed Black-winged Lovebirds are reputed to be among the gentler, less aggressive of the genus. Although named by European explorers in the early 1800s, this lovebird species was not imported to Germany until about ninety years later, in 1906. Records show that it had arrived in some British collections by 1909 and came to the United States at a later time.

ETHIOPIAN NATIVE

This lovebird is native to Ethiopia, an east African country, where it lives in open highland forests on the Ethiopian Plateau, at elevations between 3,000 and 9,000 feet. Here it lives in a variety of trees including junipers, acacias and euphorbias. They tend to congregate in small flocks and eat seeds, berries and fruits, especially figs and juniper berries.

CHARACTERISTICS

The ground color of these birds is a yellowish green. Black-winged Lovebirds are sexually dimorphic: Males and females look different. A male has a red band across his forehead, above his beak. Tiny red feathers also ring his eyes. The female does not have red feathers above her beak or around her eyes. Their beaks are red, their eyes dark brown. The feathers under their wings and their flight feathers are black. They have gray legs and a black band, or bar, at the end of their tails.

Hand-fed birds can be remarkably tame and loving with their owners, although they do not like to be hugged or handled. They will sit on a shoulder or hand, however, to get close to their owners, and they like to be talked to. Their call is a high-pitched chirping or twittering, which is not as loud as that of many of the lovebird species. In fact, their chirps have been described as enjoyable, almost musical.

The Black-winged Lovebird is also known as the Abyssinian Lovebird or the Mountain Parrot. Two pet females may not get along; these birds are territorial: They are possessive of an area they consider their own. It is not advisable to house them with birds of other species: The lovebirds may kill or break the legs or beaks of the other birds. Alone among lovebirds, females of this species pull their own chest feathers to line their nests.

Mutations are difficult to find, but reportedly, cinnamon and blue have occurred. The cinnamon mutation has brown flight feathers and lighter green feathers than normal Black-winged, but the tail band and secondary flight feathers remain black. While Black-winged Lovebirds are not as easy to find as Peach-faced, Masked and Fischer's, they are generally not priced exorbitantly. They will, however, be more expensive than normally colored birds of the three most common species.

The Black-cheeked Lovebird

The Black-cheeked Lovebird (*Agapornis nigrigenis*) is one of the larger lovebirds at 6 inches from head to tail; it weighs about 1½ ounces. In the wild, it lives in southwest Zambia amid the northern tributaries of the Zambesi River in the south-central part of the continent. Its habitat is the smallest of all the lovebirds; it prefers the river valleys at elevations of 1,800 to 3,000 feet—the lowlands of Zimbabwe.

It feeds on seeds, fruits and berries as well as leaf buds. The last of the lovebirds to be identified, it was named by W.L. Sclater in 1906. Perhaps because of its good nature, it became a popular import in the early 1900s. So many were imported at that time, however, that little attention was paid to breeding these birds in Europe, the United States and Australia. It can be difficult to find these birds today, and they are considered by some to be endangered in their small native habitat.

SPECIAL TRAITS

The Black-cheeked Lovebird has a white eye ring, and it is difficult to tell a male from a female. The ground color is green. The head, cheeks and face are brownish black, with the cheeks and face darker than the head. The dark color does not cover the entire head of this bird, as it does on the Masked Lovebird. The upper chest and nape of the neck are red-orange, and the beak is red. The legs and feet are gray.

A pure Black-cheeked Lovebird will not have blue rump feathers; these feathers will be green. Its eyes are brown. This lovebird is among the most easygoing and makes an excellent pet. It will tolerate other lovebirds and birds of other species. A blue mutation has been reported, but is not widely known. Reported mutations of this species are suspect because so many have been cross-bred (hybridized) with the Masked Lovebird. Serious breeders do not cross-breed species, understanding that they must help to maintain true species, as they appear in the wild. If one can be found, it is likely to be expensive.

This bird is also called the Black-faced Lovebird. They sound much like the Peach-faced Lovebird. Often, Black-cheeked Lovebirds, along with Red-faced and Nyasa Lovebirds, are the most expensive on the market.

The Red-faced Lovebird

The Red-faced Lovebird (*Agapornis pullaria*), first described in the 1600s, was named in 1758 and is thought to be the first lovebird imported to Europe, probably because of its large habitat, which stretches from central Africa across the continent to the west coast.

SPECIFICS

This shy, charming little bird, which was a favorite pet of upper class British women in the 1700s, is among the smallest lovebirds. It's about 5 inches from head to tail. In the wild, Red-faced Lovebirds tend to live below 4,200 feet, where they can be found in lightly wooded grasslands and more open forests and grasslands.

Wild birds tend to sleep hanging upside down in trees, and pets may surprise their owners with this habit as well. The scarcity of these birds in the pet market is due in part to their inclination to breed in termite mounds in the wild, a habitat difficult to simulate

*Red-faced
Lovebirds.*

elsewhere. Female Red-faced Lovebirds carry nesting materials in their rump feathers much like Peach-faced Lovebirds.

They eat seeds, fruits, berries and leaf buds in the wild. As you might expect of birds that like to sleep hanging upside down, these birds also hang on seed heads, eating upside down. At first glance, the Red-faced looks so similar to the Peach-faced Lovebird the two were thought to be the same species for many years. On closer inspection, however, it is more apparent that the two birds are quite different.

Red-faced Lovebirds are sexually dimorphic, but not as dramatically different as some other species: If a male and female are side by side, it is somewhat easier, but still not simple, to tell the difference between them. A male Red-faced Lovebird has red face feathers that extend from his forehead into his cheeks and throat. A female's face feathers are more orange than red and the feathers that border the red face are tinged with yellow, next to her green head and chest feathers. The male has black underwing covert feathers; the female's are green. The beaks are red, but the female's beak is more orange than that of the male. Their feet and legs are gray.

MUTATIONS

Red-faced Lovebirds are sometimes called Orange-faced Lovebirds. Although they are plentiful in their native habitat, they are rarely available in North America or Europe and can be difficult to keep alive because of their high-strung natures and need for warm temperatures. Only one color mutation has been reported that can be counted as reliable: lutino, in which the normal green color is replaced by yellow. This mutation is extremely rare.

The Black-collared Lovebird

The Black-collared Lovebird (*Agapornis swinderniana*) is so uncommon in captivity that it is unlikely any are sold as pets anymore. Native to western and central Africa, these birds are reported to live and feed in tree-tops, rarely coming to the ground. This habit makes them particularly hard to catch. Another reason they are rarely kept as pets is the largely unknown nature of their diet.

Males and females look alike. The ground color is green, with darker, more olive green feathers on the breast. On the back, or nape, of the neck the bird has a black band. The rump is blue, a band on the tail is red, the beak is black and the eyes are orange-yellow. This bird is also called Swindern's Lovebird. There are two subspecies.

CURIOUS DIET

Some maintain that they eat mainly native figs, while other say they also eat rice, insects and seeds. Black-collared Lovebirds imported to Europe as late as the 1970s did not survive quarantine. African birdkeepers report that captured Black-collared Lovebirds die after just a few days without the native figs they eat in the wild.

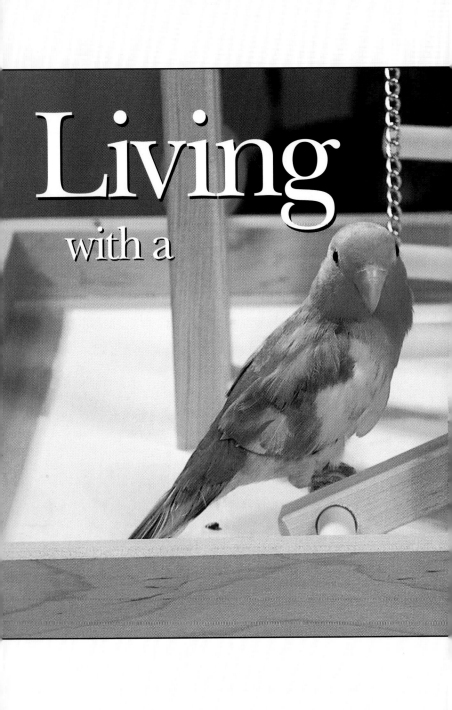

Living
with a

part two

Lovebird

chapter 4

Your Lovebird's Home

Choosing the Cage

Lovebirds thrive on activity. They need to run around, climb, chew and play constantly—certainly much more than is the norm for many larger birds. Their small size makes this need relatively easy to accommodate. Regardless of the cage you choose, remember to choose one with a strong door latch, or purchase a separate latch. Lovebirds have strong beaks and can easily pry open a door with a weak latch.

Before you buy your bird, buy her cage. Choosing the cage should take as much time as selecting the bird. This will be your bird's home. I speak from experience here. I have bought the bird and then rushed to buy the cage—

buying one that was not only unsuitable, but expensive. Despite the cost, the cage didn't last long. It was poorly made and impossible to keep clean. After that debacle, I gave a great deal of thought to the next bird cage I bought. I hope my experience will help you avoid my mistakes.

Once again, research is the key. Check all available sources of supply, including pet stores, feed stores and specialty builders that advertise in bird magazines. The guidelines are relatively simple and are based on the physical and emotional needs of lovebirds as well as their behavior.

The cage size will, of course, first depend on your budget and the size of your home. Keep in mind that lovebirds are active and love to fly and climb. They need this exercise for both their physical and mental well-being. Knowing this, choose the largest lovebird cage you can afford. Ask pet store personnel to show you cages designed specifically for lovebirds.

Your lovebird's cage should be large enough to contain toys, perches, food and water bowls and, of course, the bird.

SIZE, SHAPE AND EXTERIOR DESIGN

In general, these cages are rectangles, longer than they are wide or tall. Perches should be placed across each end, facing each other. This design allows a lovebird to fly from perch to perch in the cage. A cage about 36 inches long, 20 inches wide and 20 inches tall would be a minimum size. As you might imagine, a playpen built onto a cage is a great idea for these active clowns.

A cage that opens from the top is optimal. The cage top looks flat until you unsnap the end portions and open the top, fitting in special perches that hold the top open and form a place for the bird to sit. This is far preferable to a cage with a solid top built on it to form the permanent base of a playground. The solid base makes the cage too dark and is difficult to keep clean, an important consideration.

On the other hand, if you cannot afford such a cage, a separate playgym is portable, inexpensive and will allow your bird plenty of exercise. Cage bars for a lovebird should be horizontal, with some vertical bars in between to act as framing. The horizontal bars are critical: Lovebirds climb constantly to exercise. This kind of bar arrangement will encourage that necessary activity. Bars should be relatively close together—about ½ inch. This will prevent escapes.

A separate playgym with interesting toys will amuse your lovebird.

As you look at cages, you will see that those designed for big parrots have larger perches and the bars are spaced more widely—making it easy for a lovebird to climb right through! Also avoid cages for budgies, also called parakeets, because they are too small. Ornate cages are beautiful to look at, but they are difficult to clean. Ornate cages can also have bits of metal that stick out decoratively, which can catch a bird's foot, wing, beak or leg band, causing injury or death.

METAL IS OPTIMAL

The cage must be made of metal. The plastic, bamboo and wooden cages sold for finches are beautiful, but would be no match for a lovebird's strong beak. Your bird would be out and flying around your home in a flash. The kind of metal you choose is important, too. Choose something that will clean easily, such as chrome or stainless steel. Some metal cages come in an array of powder-coated paint colors that are attractive and easily cleaned. Avoid metals that will discolor when exposed to the fruits and vegetables your bird will throw as he eats or wipes on the bars to keep his beak clean.

If the cage is painted, be sure the paint is lead-free. Plastic coated metal bars are also unsuitable: Your bird will spend many hours stripping the plastic off the bars. While this may be fun for your bird, you will not enjoy the sight or the mess.

EASY TO CLEAN?

Because keeping your bird's cage clean is important, choose one that will be easy to work on. I always want a cage that will break down easily for regular cleaning as well as one that will allow me to clean the cage bottom in a few minutes every day without disturbing my

A cage with an easy-to-remove tray will make daily cleaning easier.

birds. That ensures that I will do the job every day, no matter what else is going on. If it's too complicated, you will be less likely to clean the cage daily and that will compromise your bird's health.

The easiest design is one with a built-in tray in the bottom of the cage. This slides out, so you can remove the soiled paper and throw it away, replacing it with a fresh lining. The drawer should be tall enough to contain the litter as you pull it out and should slide easily. Another easy-to-handle style has a snap-on bottom. To clean

47

this, you simply remove the bottom, placing the cage on top of newspapers while you work.

CAGE DOOR CHOICES

Cage doors come in three basic designs: those that open to the side, those that slide to the side or up out of the way and those that open from bottom to top, forming a porch for the bird to play on. The only door style I tend to avoid is the one that slides up to open. This door has to be secured while open, and if the curious bird plays with the latch, it will slide shut with a bang, something like a guillotine. I would avoid this kind of door.

Cage Accessories

All that activity in a lovebird cage kicks up a lot of feathers, seed hulls, bird droppings, fruit and vegetable scraps and toy parts. The busy day to day living of these little extroverts can get messy. Fortunately, some old-fashioned and some new-fangled equipment help contain this debris in the cage. Which you choose will depend as much on price as looks.

SEED GUARDS

The simple elasticized cloth "skirt" has been around for ages. You can choose this style in a variety of materials to match your home. This is washable and inexpensive, but lovebirds chew anything they can get hold of, so you should plan on replacing this, as needed.

Other seed guards are made of plastic or metal. Some cages come with plastic inserts around the edges of the cage. These will work well if they are made of sturdy plastic that will hold up against strong little beaks. Glass guards are also available, or you can have them cut for a reasonable price at a glass shop to replace any thin plastic guards that came with the cage.

Some more expensive cages come with a wide apron that flares out from the base of the cage. This is an effective way to catch debris. You may also find aprons sold alone to attach to cages. These are available through pet stores and bird magazine advertisements.

The ultimate in mess containment is an acrylic or glass cage or flight. Although you may find either at your local pet store, it is often a special-order item found in bird magazine advertisements or at bird marts, large local fairs held annually in various cities. The acrylic cage is clear on all sides, with holes drilled in the plastic to attach perches, food and water dishes and toys in various places. Companies making acrylic cages offer them in several styles. I have one that is exactly the right size for lovebirds.

If the pre-planned perch placement is not suitable, ask the manufacturer to drill more holes, where you indicate, on both ends. This can be done easily. These cages not only contain the mess, they are easily taken apart into panels, which makes them quick and simple to clean. In models I have seen, there are enough holes to allow a good exchange of air for your bird. If you have seen one you like, but would like more air holes, ask the manufacturer to modify the cage for you.

> ## SETTING UP YOUR LOVEBIRD'S CAGE
>
> Besides being safe and comfortable, you want to provide a home that is mentally stimulating to your lovebird. Try to provide the following things when picking the best cage for your pet:
>
> - A cage with a regularly shaped tray that is easy to slide in and out for frequent cleaning.
>
> - A safe cage door that opens with ease, stays securely open and has a non–"guillotine-style" door.
>
> - The largest size cage you can afford—at the minimum size 36 inches long, 20 inches wide and 20 inches tall. The bigger the better, especially if you have more than one bird.
>
> - Chrome or stainless steel metal is the safest type of cage for your bird. Wood, bamboo and plastic are not strong enough for an energetic lovebird.

If your home looks like it belongs in *House Beautiful,* and you want a lovebird, but dread the mess or worry about the way a standard cage will look, you may be in the market for a glass-sided cage or flight. These small aviaries look like pieces of furniture, and they are designed in the style of traditional, antique or modern furniture in a variety of wood. They are often hand-made, beautiful and expensive.

Natural wood branches serve as perches in many of them and the cleaning tray is hidden behind a feature that looks like a drawer. The automated ventilation system is often concealed behind carved wood. In addition, some have air-filtration systems and lights on an automatic timer. Just because a cage is expensive, however, does not mean it is better than less costly cages. It must first suit all of your bird's needs and then suit yours to be a good cage.

One thing to keep in mind with fully enclosed cages with sides of acrylic or glass: You must never place one of these cages in full sunlight or near another heat source. Under those circumstances, they will overheat and may cause the death of your bird. I own an acrylic cage that I placed away from any windows. My bird has lived in this cage for three years with no problems, and there is no litter around her cage at any time.

Of course, if you buy one of these cages, you must provide ways for your bird to climb. There are many ladders available, including at least one style that you build yourself from pre-cut pieces and those with hooks at the top to attach to perches.

Lovebirds tend to nibble on their feeding dishes— make sure that all dishes are made of ceramic or strong plastic.

DISHES

Your bird will need at least two feeding dishes and two water dishes. All must be made of ceramic or strong plastic; lovebirds have strong beaks and will gleefully destroy any made of thin plastic. If the cage you have chosen doesn't have four dishes built-in, you can buy extras to hang on the cage sides. Try them out in the store to make sure they hang correctly and can be positioned away from the perches, where the bird can't soil them with droppings. Don't plan to hang any dishes in the flight path. The more wide open this path, the better for your bird.

Perhaps the best solution for water is a bottle made for the purpose, which you can hang outside the cage. A ball bearing prevents the water from flowing freely. When the bird touches the ball with her tongue, a drop of water will come out. The biggest advantage of a water bottle is that the bird's droppings and old food will not fall into it. Anything organic that falls into the water is likely to grow bacteria—and that can cause your bird to get sick.

A water bottle keeps food and droppings out of your pet's water.

Buy at least four more dishes to replace the set in use when you clean the cage. I like to have on hand four complete sets for each of my bird cages. That way, I always have a set of clean dishes to put in my birds' cages every morning.

BATH BOWL

In addition to food dishes, buy a bathing dish or bowl. Some cages have extra openings with doors that swing out of the way. This allows you to hang the bath on the outside of the cage, flush to the wall, and still gives the bird free access from inside her cage.

The bath you buy should fit well enough that your bird cannot escape through any gaps between the bath and the cage wall. Sales personnel can help you with this. Another bath option is a wide, low-sided bowl that can sit on the bottom of the cage, away from the perches.

Keep in mind that lovebirds love bathing and will be happiest if they can do so daily.

PERCHES

The cage you choose will have perches. More than likely, they will be wooden dowels or made of plastic. Plastic perches are unacceptable, so if the cage is otherwise perfect, simply replace them. Replacement perches are usually inexpensive and buying the correct perches is one of the most important purchases you will make for your bird's home.

In the wild, birds land on a variety of branches, leaves, rocks and other natural material. They climb and they walk, which exercise their feet. They rest with one foot on the perch and one pulled up in their feathers. The variety of perching materials helps ensure healthy feet and nails. This is essential, whether the bird is wild or a pet. Except while they fly, birds are always on their feet—even when asleep.

A variety of perches, even your finger, helps keep your love-bird's feet in good condition.

Exercising their feet on perches of a variety of shapes and sizes helps keep circulation efficient and feet in good shape. The bird should not be able to wrap his feet all the way around the smallest part of the perch; on the other hand, the perch should not be so large that the bird cannot grip it firmly. Perches should be labeled for specific bird species or sizes.

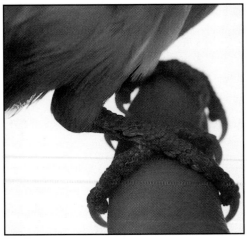

Most pet stores carry perches of such natural material as manzanita and other woods as well as dried cholla cactus skeletons. As you look at them, you will notice that the branches vary in width and have interesting twigs that your bird will enjoy chewing and bark he can strip. These perches look great, too. A cholla cactus skeleton is tubular and has many irregular holes. Your bird will enjoy chewing this and the shapes will encourage the right kind of exercise. Avoid sandpaper-covered perches and sandpaper designed to slip on perches: They can rub your bird's feet raw.

In the last few years, cement perches have come on the market—usually half perches that can be attached anywhere in the cage by a screw and wing nut. These are designed to help keep your bird's nails worn down enough to avoid the necessity of clipping them. These work to varying degrees. I have one in each of my bird's cages as an alternative to their normal perches. They are easy to clean. They come in a wide variety of colors, but I tend to stick to brown, black, green and gray—colors a bird might encounter in the wild.

As you look at the wooden perches, you may wonder if they are a waste of money. The bird, as you now know, will simply chew wood until it is sawdust. Chewing is a necessary and natural activity for parrots of any size. It gives them something interesting to do, and it keeps their beaks in the correct form. A bird's beak grows throughout his life, and the chewing keeps his beak trimmed and conditioned for splitting seeds and nuts. Perches are an important part of the bird's environment. Wooden perches are well worth the expense.

Position all perches high in the cage. Lovebirds feel most secure when they can sit toward the top of the cage. Be sure to allow enough room for your bird to sit straight, without ducking.

FLOOR COVERING

Wild birds lose feathers as they fly, bathe and groom themselves (preen). They throw food as they eat and play. Their droppings fall to the ground, generally unnoticed by them, where they are recycled and help to revitalize the earth.

A caged bird continues these activities, but the debris collects on the bottom of her cage, where it can grow mold, fungus and bacteria if not attended to regularly.

This means the floor of the cage must be covered with something to help you keep the bird's environment as clean as possible, as easily as possible. A variety of products is on the market, including sanitized bird sand, gravel covered paper and ground corn cobs or walnut shells and other bedding material. Of them all, I prefer newspaper. I have it on hand, it's nontoxic and it incurs no additional expense. (Do not use pages printed with colored inks, however. They can be toxic to your bird.)

I do not recommend bird sand because it is messy and if not changed daily, can harbor bacteria. Some bird-keepers use ground corn cobs and other bedding material on the bottom of the cage, but the temptation is to leave it too long because it tends to hide most of the debris and is expensive. Rotting food and drop-pings sitting in the bottom of the cage or mixed into these coverings will create unhealthful conditions as bacteria grows freely.

Fun with Toys

When I bought my first bird, there were few toys on the market. Today, it's great fun to cruise the aisles of even the smallest pet store, to peruse the ads in bird maga-zines and to talk to bird club enthusiasts about toys for birds. People who own and love birds are now design-ing, making and selling toys for our pets. The market has become so diverse that you will have no trouble finding just what you have in mind, including many all-natural toys.

SAFETY FIRST

Just about anything goes with toys—as long as they are safe. In her zeal to have fun, your bird will not be able to tell whether a toy is dangerous or not—that is your job. There are still too many hazardous toys on the market. I have called a number of manufacturers to complain about the danger of their toys, and often they are surprised and eager to make any changes that will help make their toys safe. If you find unsafe toys on the market, please let the manufacturers know.

Look for toys made of natural, untreated and unpainted wood. Lovebirds (and most other healthy parrots) chew. The best toy, in the view of a lovebird, is one that can be destroyed. This gives the bird an intellectual and physical activity and keeps her beak in trim. Avoid snap locks that are sometimes used to attach a toy to the top of a cage. Birds tend to get toes, legs and leg bands caught in these. If you aren't home when this happens, your bird might lose a foot or a leg or her life. If you like the toy, remove the snap attachment and replace it with a quick-link that attaches to the cage with a nut-and-bolt style closure. Quick-links are available at hardware stores.

Birds are also in danger from toys with chains whose links contain any spaces. To a bird, this looks like the perfect way to have fun—climbing on the chain. If the bird catches a body part, she will panic and thrash around, injuring herself further. Occasionally you will also see bird toys suspended from slip-on key rings. Just as keys slide easily into the groove to slide onto the ring, so can bird toes and beaks. Please replace any that are on toys you buy with quick-links. Also avoid thin plastic toys. Lovebirds will chew them and break the plastic into dangerous little pieces. Toys made of heavier acrylic are fine, and those made of brightly colored pieces that move will entertain lovebirds.

The best rule of thumb? If the toy looks dangerous, don't buy it. Look for protruding metal pieces, open spaces that could catch a small body part and anything that snaps. All of these pose potential danger. If you decide to make wooden toys yourself, buy only untreated lumber. Most lumber available at home improvement stores is pressure treated with chemicals. This makes it better for homes, but toxic to birds. Any leather you use should be treated with only natural, nontoxic products certified safe for birds.

Hanging Toys

Hanging toys of natural, untreated leather are fun for lovebirds to chew. The texture is different than wood and holds their interest. Some toys combine natural wood with knotted leather. Other great toys are made of cholla cactus skeletons, wooden beads and other wooden shapes. In addition to those toys you will find at the store, look at magazine advertisements. Several excellent toy makers sell only by direct order and they develop personal relationships with most of their customers. When you call these businesses, you often talk to the person making the toys. Some will even help you special order toys specifically for your bird's personality.

Lovebirds enjoy the playgym for climbing, swinging and interacting with their companions.

THE PLAYGYM

One toy you will find indispensable is a playgym. This should come with at least one perch. It may also have a ladder and swing. It will sit on a base to catch any droppings. Another must for a lovebird is a wooden ring that hangs from the top of his cage. Swinging is a joyous activity for these active little clowns. Remember to locate this piece of equipment carefully—away from all dangers such as overhead fans, doors, windows, heaters, the kitchen and children's play areas.

WHAT TO AVOID

When you look at supplies for your bird's cage you will see some things that are inappropriate, even though widely sold. Mite protectors certainly qualify. Pet birds rarely have mites, so these are not necessary. Perhaps more important, these protectors have dangerous chemicals in them, and it's best not to expose your bird to them. If someone tells you your bird has mites, take him to a veterinarian for expert advice. Chances are excellent that your bird does not have mites, but if so he will need professional medical care.

One of my birds had beak mites. If I had let this go or had tried to diagnose and medicate my bird myself with a mite protector or other over-the-counter medication, my bird's beak might have become severely deformed.

Never diagnose your bird's medical problems and do not use over-the-counter medications unless directed to do so by a veterinarian. If you suspect a health problem with your bird, take him to a qualified avian veterinarian.

NIGHT NIGHT

Your bird will need a cage cover. Whether you buy it or make it, this is a necessary but simple accessory. A cage cover serves several purposes. Foremost, it gives your bird a sense of security during the night, a time a bird feels instinctively vulnerable. The temperature in most homes drops at night, especially in winter. a cage cover will help protect your bird from drafts and sudden temperature changes that can stress it.

NATURAL NESTERS

Lovebirds are nest builders. If you leave any paper around, you will notice this immediately. Your bird will tear paper into strips and carry it to her

You can cover your lovebird's cage with a blanket, towel or sheet.

cage either in her beak or tucked tidily in her rump feathers. Because your lovebird cannot build a nest in her cage, provide her with a nest box. A small wooden box that attaches outside the cage is best. Your bird will sleep here in comfort, where she will feel safe and secure inside four walls. Nest boxes are readily available at pet stores. Buy the kind you can check from the outside. These have small access doors. Check the box often for cleanliness. Your bird will more than likely

57

not foul it with droppings. If the box becomes dirty at any time, though, replace it.

Cage Placement

Where you put the cage in your home is as important as the cage itself. Lovebirds are social creatures. Like all birds, they feel best when they are members of a flock. You will become the bird's flock when you bring him home with you. He will love being around you, watching you go about your daily activities. Place the cage in a room where you spend a great deal of your leisure time, such as the family room. The best place to locate the cage is next to the wall, so the bird doesn't have to worry about constant, unpredictable activity all around his home. This will help calm your bird and give him some much-needed security.

If you can, place the cage in a corner to give it two solid sides. You can also place nonpoisonous house plants near the cage, recognizing that the bird may chew them from time to time. The cage should be at about your chest height to give the bird a greater sense of security. You can either place the cage on a tall chest or a four-legged table, or you can hang it from the ceiling. Old-fashioned stands made to hang cages are generally unsuitable because they can be tipped over easily.

A room with enough windows to let in plenty of natural light would be ideal, although you should avoid putting your bird directly in front of a window, where direct sunlight could overheat the bird. Hand-fed birds retain many instincts you will be surprised to observe. An instinctive fear of predatory birds, cats and other animals he can see through the window may terrify

SETTING UP HOUSE

- Your lovebird craves companionship—put her home near the hub of family activity.

- Placing the cage near a wall or in a corner creates a feeling of safety and security for your bird.

- Avoid putting the cage in direct sunlight or in draughts—moderate and consistent temperature is best.

- Arrange the cage in a room with a television or radio; background noise keeps your lovebird company when you are out of the room.

- The cage should be at your chest height to add to a sense of security.

your bird. Such stress could lead to illness. Make sure all windows have secure screens to prevent your bird from flying outside.

Place the cage away from a door that leads to the outside, which could allow in drafts. Another important consideration for cage placement is heat/air-conditioning ducts and registers. If a cage is near any of these the bird could overheat or become too cold when the heat or air-conditioning is on. Always place a bird cage away from these and any other sources of air flow. Any abrupt or extreme change in temperature can stress your bird and make him more susceptible to illness.

A room equipped with a radio, stereo system or television is also a plus. The noise will help your bird's sense of well-being, especially when you are gone. In the wild, animals are noisy when all is well. When a predator approaches, birds and other smaller animals take cover and remain as quiet as they can. Instinctively, most birds feel less secure when it is quiet.

The worst place to locate a cage is the kitchen. With its fumes, likelihood of drastic changes of temperature and dangers from open cooking pots and pans, this is truly a potential disaster area for birds. In short, keep your bird out of the kitchen.

Indoor Aviaries

If you have the room, an indoor aviary could be a wonderful alternative to a cage, especially for a pair of lovebirds. Ideally, this aviary should be about 4 to 6 feet long and 3 feet wide. It can be as tall as your ceiling or lower, if you wish. The top of the aviary should be approximately 2 feet taller than the door into the enclosure. Lovebirds tend to fly up when frightened, and this will help to ensure that they will not fly out the door when you walk in to clean. To ensure that cleaning is as easy as possible, the door should be tall enough to enter without stooping.

As in a cage, you should provide many perches of natural material at opposite ends of the aviary. Place food

dishes up high on the walls of the aviary to avoid contamination from droppings. The floor must be washable. If you can, install a drain in the center and slope
the floors toward the drain.

To make the aviary attractive, you can add nontoxic
plants, realizing that the birds will destroy them with
great enthusiasm. Another option is to position nontoxic plants around the outside of the aviary, out of the
reach of your birds.

chapter 5

Caring for Your Lovebird

A lovebird needs quality care every day to keep him healthy and in good spirits. Birds are most well adjusted when they feel safe and comfortable in a pleasant environment. The importance of routine care cannot be stressed too often. An established daily routine will save you time, and will ensure your bird's health and happiness.

Cleaning House

Every day, you should clean the bottom of your bird's cage, changing the cage floor covering. Hot soap and water will help kill most bacteria. If you feel the need for a stronger cleaner, you can use a 10 percent bleach and

90 percent water solution. Rinse anything dipped in this solution thoroughly before returning it to the bird's cage.

Once a week, you should thoroughly clean your lovebird's cage. This task can be made easier by placing the cage in the shower and rinsing it with hot water from the shower faucet. Always be sure to take your lovebird, his water bottle and food dishes, the tray liner and the bird's toys out of the cage before putting the dirty cage into the shower. After hot water has rinsed the cage for a short while, you can then use some steel wool or a toothbrush to scrub off any stuck-on debris. When the cage looks clean, you can disinfect the cage with a spray-on disinfectant that is nontoxic to birds. Remember to carefully read the instructions before applying a disinfectant.

Before you return your lovebird and his accessories to the cage, be sure to rinse the cage thoroughly and dry it well. Wooden perches can be dried quickly in a hot oven for about ten minutes. The perches should be completely cool before they are put back in the cage.

Exchange all dishes with clean ones filled with fresh clean seed, water and soft food. A few hours after you put cooked food in the cage, remove it. When you clean the cage, look at the bird's droppings. Are they the same color as usual? Are they firm and round, with green on the outside and white on the inside? Are there about as many as usual? Did the bird eat well— about as much as he usually does? This inspection will soon become second nature to you, but is often the first clue to the state of your bird's health.

When the Weather Changes

It is important to be aware of the seasonal changes and their effect on your lovebird. Keep your bird cool by keeping her out of direct sunlight and offering her plenty of fresh, juicy fruits and crisp vegetables. Remember to remove any uneaten food promptly, to prevent your pet from eating something that has spoiled. A gentle mist of water from a clean spray bottle is another great way to cool your bird on a hot day.

When it gets cool outside, remember to keep your lovebird comfortable as well. Watch out for drafty spots in the house and avoid placing your pet's cage near them. A heavier cage cover may help keep your bird warmer, especially at night when the temperature tends to drop.

The daily bath can be great fun for your lovebird.

Grooming and Bathing

In the wild, healthy birds are all well-groomed. Keeping your bird well-groomed is easy. Most lovebirds really appreciate a daily bath. Offer tepid water in a shallow wide-mouth bowl with straight sides or a saucer that can hold about ½ inch of plain water. Never add soap or conditioner to the bath water, even though some are available. These additions could damage the surface of the bird's feathers, altering her ability to keep warm or repel water.

Place the bath in the cage first thing in the morning. If your bird seems reluctant to bathe, you can put wet iceberg or Romaine lettuce leaves on a plate for him to wallow in. If this doesn't appeal to your bird, you can spray him with a fine mist. Of my three birds, one prefers to shower with my husband, one runs up and down the kitchen counter begging for a mist bath each day and the third bathes in a straight-sided dish. You will soon discover your bird's preferences. Cater to them. Bathing encourages preening the feathers.

Grooming is an essential part of a healthy lovebird's daily routine, both in the wild and in your home. Bathing will remove any dirt or food from your bird's feathers and will encourage your bird to preen, an essential grooming technique that birds must perform daily to keep their feathers in top condition. It has also been proven in several species, including lovebirds, that daily bathing, especially where there is low humidity, can help prevent birds from beginning to pull, or pluck, their own feathers.

Bathing a lovebird is usually simple; they love water and most will bathe willingly in a shallow saucer, a commercial bird bath hung outside the cage or a straight-sided bowl placed in the bottom of the cage. Most also enjoy frolicking in the spray of a misting bottle. Some are reluctant, however. A few little tricks can turn them into enthu-

Lightly mist your lovebird with water to encourage the idea of bathing.

siastic bathers, too. Lovebirds enjoy large green leaves of Romaine lettuce, spinach or bok choy cabbage. To encourage your lovebird to bathe, soak some of these leaves in cold water. Put the wet leaves on the bottom of the cage on top of clean paper towels or on the kitchen counter and allow your bird to explore. Soon, he will frolic in the water on the leaves. If even this fails, use a misting bottle filled with warm water.

It is a good idea to have bath time for your lovebird early in the day to allow ample time for his feathers to dry. You can bond with your pet by wrapping him loosely in a towel and gently drying his feathers. You might also use the lowest setting on your blow dryer when there is cool weather, to keep your lovebird from catching a chill. Remember to keep the blow dryer moving at all times so your bird doesn't get too hot!

BEAK AND NAIL TRIMMING

A healthy bird's beak shouldn't need trimming. If your bird's beak suddenly begins to overgrow, take her to your vet immediately. This could be a sign of ill health. Do not try to trim a bird's beak. A vein in the beak could easily be clipped.

> **WATCH OUT FOR WARM WEATHER**
>
> When the weather gets warm, you may notice that you perspire more. Unfortunately, your bird doesn't perspire. Your lovebird cools off by sitting with her wings held away from her body, rolling her tongue and holding her mouth open. Watch out for your bird in warm weather because she can quickly overheat and may suffer from heatstroke, which requires immediate veterinary care. If you are living in a warm climate, check with your local avian veterinarian for tips to protect your bird from this potentially serious problem.

If you have provided a variety of perches in different shapes and widths, your lovebird's toenails should wear to the proper length naturally. If the bird's nails grow too long, though, they could become a danger—catching in cloth and tearing into the vein, which could bleed excessively. Talk to your vet about the proper length and how to clip them if necessary. If your bird has light colored nails, you can see the vein and avoid it. If your bird has dark nails, though, you cannot see the vein; avoiding it comes with practice.

Recovering a Lost Bird

Because lovebirds enjoy flying so much and need the exercise, many experts recommend that they should be allowed to fly every day. A lovebird whose wings have not been clipped is a strong flyer. The danger

If you allow your lovebird to fly, make sure that all windows and doors are closed and you have birdproofed the house.

here is that she could fly out a window or door that has been left open. Lovebirds are so small, that it is all too possible to walk out a door, forgetting the bird is on your shoulder until she is frightened by the outdoor experience and flies away.

IF YOUR LOVEBIRD ESCAPES

- Keep a tape of your bird's calls to play outside to tempt your bird back to her home.

- Set your bird's cage in your front or backyard with her favorite treats nearby as a lure.

- Use another caged bird to catch your lovebird's attention.

- Let your veterinarian know that your lovebird is lost. Alert local animal shelters and other veterinary offices as well.

- Put fliers up in your community with a description of your bird as well as your phone number and a reward. You can also place an add in your neighborhood newspaper.

- Don't give up hope.

While it's difficult to recover a lost bird, it's not impossible. It's possible now to have an encoded microchip placed under your bird's skin. If the bird is captured by someone else, he or she can have the chip read to determine who the owners are. You could also have your bird tattooed.

Other methods of retrieval include taping your bird's calls and playing them loudly outside to attract the bird back to you or to his cage, which is placed away from people, fully stocked with food and treats. The best solution, though, is prevention.

Set up regular free-flight times and make sure all windows and doors are closed before your bird comes out. If your bird is out and on your shoulder all day, teach yourself to put the bird in his cage and double check before walking out the door. I've done this with several free flying birds and have not lost one since my budgies flew away when I was a teenager. If you are absent minded, perhaps an indoor flight is the answer.

chapter 6

Feeding Your Lovebird

When I first began keeping birds, it was generally thought that birds needed only seeds in their diet. Over the years, my birds taught me that they wanted what I ate. Because I am indulgent with my pets, I allowed them to eat "people food," including vegetables, fruit, cheese and meat.

In the last fifteen years, avian veterinarians have become increasingly interested in formulated, or pelleted, foods for birds. As these have improved, I have added them to my birds' diets as well. Today, avian veterinarians and aviculturists work together to devise the most nutritious diet for pet birds. This is no simple task. So many species are kept as pets, and the needs of each are different.

Diet in the Wild

One way to determine what to feed a bird is to observe wild birds of a species to see what they eat. This is a good start, but by no means a perfect solution to the problem. Wild birds fly when approached, leaving the observer to guess what they've eaten. Perhaps more important, it would be impossible to keep a flock of wild birds in sight for any extended period of time, and who knows what they might eat while out of sight.

Wild lovebirds have been observed eating a variety of seeds, including grass, millet, wheat, rice and other seeds and grains. They also eat corn, figs, berries, guavas and other fruits as well as leaf buds, insects and insect larvae. The key word is variety.

Avian Nutrition

We understand that humans need a variety of foods to take in proper amounts of protein, carbohydrates and fats to maintain our bodily growth and energy requirements. The same is true of birds. Because no one food supplies all of the nutrients for good health, an assortment must be offered. In this way, a bird will be more likely to eat enough of the various nutrients he needs.

Your healthy lovebird will thrive on a diet with a balance of protein, carbohydrates and fat.

Monitoring the Diet

Keep track of what your bird eats. You may want to use a notebook for this purpose. Each bird will have his or her likes and dislikes. After about six months, you may see a pattern developing. If your bird simply will not eat one or two of the mixes you make up, you can either continue offering them for another six months to see if the bird will eventually try these seeds, or you can stop ordering them. If your bird eats only one or two kinds of the seed, though, continue offering all the seeds. She may eventually convert to a more balanced eating pattern.

Your record of what your bird eats will help you in another dramatically important way. Poor appetite may be the first sign of illness. If you know with certainty what and how much your bird eats each day, you will notice immediately when something is wrong, before he gets to a critical stage.

SEEDS

Offer your lovebird millet as a special treat a couple times a week.

Most aviculturists believe seeds form the basis of a wild lovebird's diet; therefore, we should offer a good quality seed mix. When you shop for seeds at a well-stocked pet store or feed market, you will notice there are large seeds and small. It is best to buy an assortment of seeds and mix them yourself. Every day, offer your lovebird a mix of the following seeds: niger, hemp, silver millet (not on the branch), buckwheat, flax, peas and oat, to which you add a budgie mix and a canary mix.

Millet sprays can be offered as a treat about every two or three days. If offered every day, your lovebird will eat them to the exclusion of everything else, something like a child who has unlimited access to candy.

Sunflower seeds are large seeds, which you can add separately at a rate of about six a day. As you will soon find, there are three types of sunflower seeds: black, striped and white. Each contains different nutrients. Not so long ago, sunflower seeds were considered too fatty for birds, and many people quit offering them to their birds altogether. These seeds do contain valuable nutrition, but should be offered in limited quantity so the bird will eat other seeds, too.

Sprouting

It's critical to use fresh seed because it contains the most nutrients. You can easily find out if seed is fresh by trying to sprout it. Cut a piece of a new sponge. Put it in a small bowl of water until it has absorbed the water. Place the wet sponge on a small plate in the sun and sprinkle some seeds on the top, working them into the holes of the sponge. Keep the sponge damp and fresh seeds will sprout. Do not feed these to your bird because you have not controlled the possible growth of bacteria or mold.

Sprouted seeds are a valuable addition to any bird's diet. Sprouting them is easy, but must be done carefully. The best candidates are millet, wheat, oat and sunflower seeds.

For one or two birds, place a tablespoon of seeds in a bowl.

Fresh sprouts are a tasty addition to your lovebird's diet.

Cover them with tepid water. Cover the bowl and leave it for about twelve hours in a warm home or twenty-four hours in a cold home. Rinse the seeds well, looking carefully for any that are oozing a liquid or look as if they may have fungi or mold growing on them. If many in the batch are spoiled, throw them all out.

Dry the seeds between multiple layers of paper towels, and then feed them to your birds. Throw away any they do not eat in about four hours to avoid the possibility of digestive upsets due to spoiled food.

FRUITS AND VEGETABLES

Seeds, of course, do not a balanced diet make; fruits and vegetables are a necessary addition. The only members of this group you should not offer your bird are avocado and rhubarb leaves. Between the seed and the meat and between the skin and the meat is a toxin that can kill a bird. Otherwise, pick and choose; this

71

can be great fun. Do avoid all seed pits and apple seeds, which are potentially toxic to birds. Some of my birds' favorite fruits included pears, plums, apricots, apples, figs, passion fruit, strawberries, blackberries, raspberries, pomegranates, bananas, cherries and grapes.

Among the vegetables that are the most popular among my flock are Brussels sprouts, jalapeño peppers, red bell peppers with seeds, Chinese pea pods, English pea pods, broccoli, chicory, dandelion (purchased at the grocery store to avoid any pesticides and fertilizers wild dandelions may have been exposed to), corn on the cob, carrots, beet greens, chickweed, spinach, tomatillos, sour cucumbers, parsley and chicory. Avoid iceberg lettuce and any other pale lettuce; they offer little or no nutritional value, outside of water and fiber. The same is true of eggplant.

Feeding your lovebird fruit is a refreshing way to provide essential vitamins.

If you have a season when fresh fruits are unavailable at reasonable prices, you can offer dried fruits. To make them more appealing, soak them. Discard them on the same schedule you use for fresh or cooked food.

FUN WITH FOOD

Lovebirds relish leafy vegetables. One way to make your bird a special treat is to rinse lettuce leaves in cold water just prior to hanging them in the cage. Your bird will react with delight. Right at the top of your lovebird's hit list are eating, playing and bathing in water, making this combination a double treat. Your delighted bird will rub against the wet leaves to take a bath, perhaps nibbling as she does so.

Know What to Throw Away

Depending on the temperature in the house, I discard the food either four hours (in summer) or seven to eight hours (on cool winter days) after placing it in the cage. If it begins to smell too fruity or ripe in your home, throw away the food. There will be waste and plenty of it. Wild birds eat only part of each thing they try, and your bird's habits will be the same. It will not be economical to try to recycle this food and give it to your bird again, however. Spoiled food can cause your bird to become ill, and a visit to the vet can be traumatic and expensive.

CLEAN FOOD IS A MUST

Several years ago, a pair of my birds came down with a disease called klebsiella. For me, the most difficult part was figuring out how they got this and why the birds remained sick, despite excellent care from a top-notch avian vet. We tested the water to be sure I didn't have bacteria in my water pipes. Then our wonderful vet asked me to have the fruits and vegetables tested.

Although I had bought them at a good market, the test results were dismaying. The food showed the presence of mice and roach droppings, as well as other unhealthful bacteria. While I was repulsed, the vet explained that most fresh food will be contaminated as it grows and while it is stored near the fields or even in warehouses that service local markets.

> **WHEN FEEDING YOUR LOVEBIRD FRUIT...**
>
> Remove cherry pits and apple seeds, both of which could cause illness. As a general rule of thumb, remove seeds and pits from most fruits because they may be toxic. Exceptions are those that have tiny seeds like raspberries, strawberries, boysenberries and kiwi fruit. You should not offer your bird avocado or rhubarb leaves because they contain a toxin that is harmful to birds.

Scrubbing the skin of such food with liquid dish soap and water will suffice in most instances. You must be sure to rinse the vegetables well to remove any soap, dirt or bacteria. Dry them with paper towels and store as usual in your refrigerator. This will be enough for most healthy, unstressed birds.

People Food

Lovebirds need protein and calcium for good health. Although they can get some in fruits and vegetables, it's best to offer such good sources as cheese, egg and commercial egg food (sold at pet and feed stores). My birds enjoy cheddar cheese, jack cheese, scrambled or boiled egg, steak, hamburger, pork and pork bones and chicken and chicken bones. They also demand baked (or microwaved) sweet potatoes, squash, pasta and cooked rice. I often cook a batch of kidney beans, split peas, pinto beans or pink beans for my birds. Some birdkeepers cook a mixture of dried beans to feed their birds once a day.

In short, they eat what we eat, with the exception of avocado, rhubarb leaves, chocolate, alcohol and large portions of dairy products. Birds do not have the enzyme necessary to digest dairy products; however, if we forget to offer a little cheese or egg, a din of shrieking is our reward. Believe me, we always knuckle under and give them the food.

My menu planning tends to take into account their tastes as well as ours. In addition to their seeds and fresh fruits and veggies, they may eat cooked oatmeal, French toast, pancakes or eggs for

Your bird will look forward to mealtime if you provide a variety of interesting foods.

breakfast. For lunch, they get a sample of whatever sandwich or cheese and crackers we eat. At dinnertime, they begin to take note of what I'm cooking. If it's a favorite, you can hear them next door. We eat at the same time as our birds, like the flock we have become. They eat in or on their cages, though, because human saliva can make a bird sick. Each of us has his or her own plate or dish, including the birds.

Formulated, or Pelleted, Food

Nutrition is a major concern with all of us, but it is of particular concern to avian veterinarians. Despite a much longer expected life span in the wild, the average pet bird lives only about five years. The cause of death is often malnutrition. To help alleviate this problem, many bird food companies and veterinarians have worked on formulating pellets to meet the nutritional needs of various species of birds. Check with your avian veterinarian on types and qualities available.

To help ensure good overall nutrition and prevent boredom, I do not offer pelleted food alone. I offer it each day in addition to seeds, fruits and vegetables and cooked foods. My reasoning is that wild birds eat a huge variety of foods, which helps them to obtain all of the nutrition they need. Aside from nutrition, which I doubt my birds think of, I want to allay boredom. If I had to eat the same thing every day, no matter how nutritious, I'm sure my interest would drop dramatically.

Watching birds eat can be great fun. They rip into their food, throw it, wipe it all over cage bars and perches, stand on it and feed it to each other (and will offer it to you, too). For a bird, food is fun. Birds are no better than most humans, though, at choosing to eat a balanced diet of what is best for them. So, I offer a wide variety of foods and hope that what they eat of each will help them ingest a balanced diet. My birds are rarely sick and none show signs of slowing down. I expect that they will all live to ripe old ages. Why? Good nutrition.

When and How to Feed Your Bird

Make fresh, healthful food available to your bird all day and into the evening. Lovebirds are tiny, but they metabolize food quickly. Their digestive systems are small, which means they cannot eat much at one time, but will need to eat many times a day. The amount of food one healthy lovebird consumes during the day will surely surprise you.

Develop a regular schedule for feeding your bird. She is completely dependent on you for food and will feel more secure if she knows when she will eat each day.

An added benefit is that you will be sure to feed your bird and will remove food before it spoils. If you work either in or out of your home and find the morning already rushed, fix the fruits and veggies the night before and keep them in the refrigerator until the next morning when you give them to your bird. You can give the bird the fresh seed and water just before you put him to bed.

If the perches are placed correctly in the cage, food should remain unsoiled throughout the night. Share some of your breakfast and dinner food with your bird, including fruit, vegetables and meat. If you are home for lunch, you can share that, too.

Be patient when offering your bird new foods—it may take a while for him to take a nibble.

When you replace seed each day, don't assume that because the seed dish looks full it is. Lovebirds discard the seed hulls, or outer coverings, as they eat, and most of the hulls will fall back into the dish, making it look full. You can blow out hulls and then mix in new seed if your bird hasn't fouled his dish with droppings or cooked or fresh food.

Wash the dishes in the dishwasher before using them again. When you offer your bird new foods, he may at first reject them. This is normal and probably based on an instinct to avoid unknown foods, which could be poisonous. Hand-fed birds usually adapt to new foods with greater ease than parent-fed birds. Nevertheless, with either kind of bird, continue to offer new foods.

Your bird may reject the food for six months or several years. In the end, he will eventually try it and may find a new favorite. My birds are especially prone to try new foods when they can see us eat the foods, too.

Vitamins

A lot of what makes nutritional sense for humans makes equal sense for birds. If your bird eats a varied, balanced diet, she does not need supplemental vitamins. If you think your bird needs them, check with your avian veterinarian before you buy the supplements.

Never put vitamin drops in your bird's drinking water. It can make the water unpalatable and may spoil before you change the water. In all my years of birdkeeping, I have never given my birds supplemental vitamins. The dangers from overdosing on various vitamins are many and easily avoided.

More Things to Avoid

Do not pick wild grass seeds, leaf buds or branches for your bird. These could have been sprayed with insecticides or herbicides, both of which are toxic. If you garden organically, you can feed your birds food from your garden. If you use any kind of pesticide or systemic fertilizer, do not feed food from your garden to your bird.

In the past, aviculturists and veterinarians often recommended that we offer our birds *cuttlebone* and *grit*. In Europe and Australia, many birdkeepers continue this practice. In the United States, however, *both are often recommended against.*

Keeping Your **Lovebird** Healthy

Lovebirds can live a long life with lots of good care and loving companionship. Unfortunately, many small birds are not given the opportunity to live a long time because their owners may be reluctant to take them to the veterinarian. The best chance you can give your lovebird to enjoy a full, healthy life is to find a competent avian veterinarian.

Quarantine— What It Is and How to Do It

When you bring a new lovebird into your home, you should quarantine the bird. Although standard practice cited by many birdkeepers is to quarantine a new bird for twenty-one days, it is better to keep her separate from your birds for ninety days. Some bird diseases can take that long to develop. Quarantine must be strict. Put the new bird in a separate room and never mingle the perches, toys or food and water dishes with those that belong to your other birds. Wash all food dishes in the dishwasher. Wash your hands carefully before handling your older bird, and always dry them on paper towels. When you first buy the new bird, have your avian vet give her a thorough checkup. Have one more set of blood tests and feces cultures run after the ninety day quarantine.

Choosing a Veterinarian

Choosing a veterinarian is one of the most important tasks you will undertake for your bird. Preferably a qualified avian veterinarian, the vet must be knowledgeable about birds. How do you find one?

If you have joined or visited a lovebird club, members will have recommendations. The pet store or breeder from whom you buy the bird may also be able to advise you. If these methods fail, you can all a veterinarian and ask who in the area is qualified to treat birds. Most areas have wild bird rehabilitators who will be happy to advise you on who in your area is the best. This latter method is how I found my avian veterinarian when I made my last move. Out of curiosity, I also asked the veterinarian who treats my dogs to recommend an avian veterinarian. She gave me the same name as had the wild bird rehabilitator. That certainly made me feel confident about the vet!

WHEN TO SEE AN AVIAN VETERINARIAN

You should take your bird for her first visit shortly after you buy her—preferably on your way home. That means you will have researched and located the best vet prior to buying the bird.

Thereafter, you should take the bird in once a year for a well-bird checkup to keep your vet familiar with you and your bird. This checkup should also uncover subtle problems that are not obvious to you. Ask the vet to do a thorough blood screen and fecal culture.

Otherwise, you should call your avian vet at the first sign of illness or in case of injury such as broken bones or serious burns. Make an appointment and take the bird in for a checkup. Remember, an avian vet is one who is familiar with birds. A vet who sees mostly cats and dogs will not be able to treat a sick bird or determine if a bird has health problems.

PREPARING FOR THE FIRST VISIT

On your first visit, ask plenty of questions. Some you might include are: "Do you take continuing education courses in avian veterinary medicine?" "Are you a certified avian veterinarian?" "How many birds do you see each week?" "Are lab tests done in-house or sent out?" "Who sees my bird if he is injured or becomes ill on a weekend or after hours?" If you are not satisfied with the answers, continue looking now. Don't wait until your bird is ill.

Signs of Illness

In the wild, an animal that is weakened by injury or illness is the first one a predator will choose to attack. From the predator's point of view, it makes good sense. This animal will be easier to catch than a healthy member of the group. Probably for this reason, birds instinctively hide signs of illness. It's not a conscious decision; some survival behaviors, including this one, occur spontaneously. It's not impossible, though, for an alert owner to spot signs of illness long before anyone else can.

I got up one morning and noticed a slightly dazed look in my normally rambunctious bird's eyes. Doodle is normally alert and full of attitude. Because reaching my vet was quite a drive, I made an appointment right away and brought Doodle's mate along, as well. I reasoned that if Doodle were ill, Yankee would be soon. They fed each other, bathed in the same bowl, ate the same food and slept nestled close together. At first glance, my vet, who is an experienced avian veterinarian, was mystified by my assertion that Doodle was ill.

To him, she looked fine. Lab tests, though, revealed an infection. Because we caught it in time, Doodle recovered quickly and has been healthy ever since.

Preventive Care

The way to spot illness before it becomes obvious is to know exactly what your bird looks like and acts like when he is well. Lovebirds are dynamic little creatures. They will call to you and fly around the room looking for mischief. If the level of activity is slower than normal, look for other signs.

When looking for signs of illness, take the whole bird into consideration. Activity level is just one factor. Look for reasons the bird might be slower than normal. Is it much colder in the house than usual? Hotter? Do you have visitors? Are there any other changes to the bird's physical surroundings, such as balloons brought in for a party or a new light fixture? Birds are wary of altered environments and will watch cautiously to be sure the modification doesn't mean danger.

Each day, as you change the covering on the bottom of your bird's cage, notice what his droppings look like. They should be firm and round, green on the outside and white on the inside. Loose yellowish or bright green droppings, for instance, are not normal. All white droppings indicate trouble, too, as do those that are red or blackish.

CONTACT YOUR VETERINARIAN RIGHT AWAY IF...
your lovebird exhibits warning signs of illness including
• a change in activity level
• silence (your bird isn't calling or singing)
• weight loss
• no interest in food or treats
• lethargy
• difficulty moving about the cage
• a change in normal appearance of droppings
• drooping wings
• labored, wheezing breathing
• nasal discharge
• swollen, tired, dull, runny eyes
• regurgitated food
• extensive inactivity and fluffed feathers
• resting for long periods of time on the cage bottom
• odd shaped feathers
• excessive scratching and bald patches
• lumps on its body

Again, though, look at the whole picture before jumping to a conclusion. If the bird has eaten lots of fruits or vegetables of those colors, his droppings will reflect this. So, if your bird's droppings are tinted with red, but the bird is active, his eyes are bright and clear and he has eaten beets or other red food, the beets are probably the cause of the unusual droppings. Keep an eye on him, though, to watch for a return to normal.

Look carefully at your bird each day, several times a day, to become familiar with what he looks like at various times of the day. Make a mental note of the time he normally awakens. When is he active or inactive during the day? Most birds wake up early in the morning and are active until afternoon, when they take naps. They awaken again in time for the family dinner and will remain active until bedtime. If you work swing shift or a nighttime shift, often your bird will adjust his schedule to suit your active times. Always be sure, though, that your bird gets about ten to twelve hours of sleep at night.

Get to know your lovebird's routine, including when he naps and when he's most active.

Each time you remove your bird's seed, water and fresh food, take a good look at what she has eaten and how much she drank. Also check to see if she has fouled her drinking water with droppings or food. If there are droppings in the water, move some perches or relocate the dish. If there is food in the water, relocate the water dish away from the fresh food dish.

How much does she eat daily? Make a mental note. The amount eaten each day is another good indicator of your bird's general health and well-being. The first few days at home, your bird may not eat much. She is still adjusting to her surroundings. Base your assessment of what she should eat on the days after she has adjusted to living with you. In general, if your bird is inactive and sleeping much more than is normal, if she is eating less, if her droppings are loose or discolored, if her eyes are dull or if she sits listlessly on her perch with feathers fluffed, she is sick.

How to Maintain Good Health

A lovebird that eats a nutritious, well-balanced diet and is kept in clean surroundings is a hardy little pet. Giving your pet healthful food will not be difficult, but may require you to change some habits. The effort that goes into taking good care of a lovebird, though, will result in a more healthful environment for all of the inhabitants, including you!

Cleanliness cannot be overstated. In addition to keeping your bird's cage and all accessories clean, you must pay special attention to the food preparation areas of your kitchen, from the counters to the sinks. Of course, there is the obvious—if you handle raw beef, pork or chicken, you must use an antibacterial cleaner on anything it might have touched, including your hands.

Never use a wooden chopping block to cut up fruits and vegetables if you have also used it to cut meat. For bird food, I always use the same cutting board—one made of plastic. Each time I use it, I wash it in the dishwasher. Also wash sponges in the dishwasher and use only paper towels; dish- and washcloths can harbor bacteria, even if freshly laundered.

Do not offer your bird any food you have had in your mouth—don't even bite off a section and then give it to your bird. Other food problems include food kept at improper temperatures or moldy food. If there is any doubt about the safety of the food, throw it away. A small amount of mold on a food is like the tip of the iceberg. What you can't see can still be dangerous and cause your bird to become ill.

> ## A SIMPLE SOLUTION
>
> To keep seeds fresh and prevent seed moths, freeze any seeds as soon as you bring them into your home. If you open the bag before freezing it, the moths will quickly escape. When you take the bag out of the freezer, put it in a closed container such as a large jar or a plastic storage bag. Seal the bag or jar as soon as you put the seeds inside, and keep it sealed until the container is room temperature.

Test the freshness of seed periodically by trying to grow it in a new damp sponge. If it won't grow, it isn't fresh. Throw it away and seek a new source. Seed moths can be a problem. If you suddenly notice a lot of small, beige moths flying around your home and collecting on the ceiling, suspect seed moths. While these are not dangerous to you or to your bird, they are an annoyance.

Set up a schedule and stick to it. You will find that it becomes an ingrained habit and takes only a small part of your daily and weekly time to keep your bird's environment clean.

AIRBORNE TOXINS

Birds have sensitive lungs, and many things we use around the house as a matter of course can be toxic to birds. Nonstick coatings on pots and pans, for instance, can emit fumes that will kill birds if overheated—to about 536° Fahrenheit. While this requires misuse of the pans, it occurs often enough that I gave away all of my nonstick pans. This prevents house guests from using them to broil in or forgetting they had left a burner on under one. This relieves my mind.

Other sources of toxic fumes include paint and most insecticides. Most of us have our homes sprayed for insects. Before you do so, ask the company you plan to use to certify that the chemicals it uses are nontoxic to birds. When I moved to Houston, where spraying is a must, it took some time to find a company, but my birds are healthy, which makes my effort worthwhile. Any spray with a potential for toxicity to human children will certainly be toxic to birds.

Other problem substances include most things that come in spray bottles, such as clothes starch, cooking oil, hair spray, pesticides, herbicides, oven cleaner, house paint, spot remover, deodorants, perfume, shellac, suntan lotions and flea bombs. Often the propellant is as dangerous as the contents of the can.

Some products can endanger birds simply by being in the house. These products emit gases toxic to birds and should not be used with the bird in the house. If you must use these products, take your bird to a friend's home or leave him overnight at the vet's office until you can rid your home of the fumes. These products include chlorine, formaldehyde, acrylics, diazanon, drain cleaner, floor polish, gasoline, kerosene, house paint, paint remover, shoe polish, nail polish, bleach, nail polish remover, felt-tip markers, mothballs, shellac, lye, permanent solution and flea collars.

This is not a total list. Be suspicious of anything that emits an odor, except food. It should go without saying that all of these substances are toxic if your bird eats them.

HUMANS CAN BE A HEALTH HAZARD, TOO

As much as you love your bird, you can still be hazardous to his health. A few precautions will remedy the situation.

If you smoke, please do not do so in the house. Secondhand smoke is dangerous to birds, and tobacco is poisonous. If you leave cigarettes lying around and your bird eats some, she could die. If you drink, do not allow your bird to join you. If she likes to drink from a glass, offer her a clean glass of water or juice. Never allow a bird to drink alcohol.

Your mouth is home to many bacteria harmful to your bird. Do not allow your bird to touch your tongue or teeth with her beak or tongue. Do not share food that has been in your mouth. If you kiss your bird, plant the kiss firmly on the front of her beak or on the top of her head. This will keep your saliva away from the bird's mouth.

If you want to kiss your lovebird, only kiss the front of her beak or the top of her head.

When you visit pet stores, bird shows or a friend who owns a bird, change clothes, shower and wash your hair before you handle your bird. Many viruses and bacteria can be carried on your skin, hair or clothing. If your bird comes into contact with these viruses, he could become ill. For this reason, I do not let people whose birds I am unsure of (I am not positive they are healthy) handle my birds.

Household Danger Areas

The two most dangerous rooms in your home will probably be the kitchen and the bathroom. Cooking spray and other fumes as well as cooking food present a major danger to your little bird. If lovebirds were not so curious and intelligent, they might not get into as much trouble in these rooms as they do. However, a little forewarning will help you prevent disaster. While you cook, lock your bird in his cage. Hot appliances, food, steam, constantly changing temperatures and fumes all combine to make the kitchen a hazardous place for birds.

One of my birds flew into a pot of soup years ago. He had flown around my kitchen for thirteen years, and I was sure he knew all of its hazards. Flying through the steam of the soup, though, made his wings too heavy and he fell in. I quickly immersed him in cool (not cold) water, which stopped the burn, but the shock combined with his age caused him to die. I still feel awful about that accident—mostly because it was due to my carelessness.

Bathrooms are equally dangerous. Again, they are filled with toxic substances such as deodorants, cleaners and perfumes. The most deadly part of the bathroom is standing water in the toilet or sink. Many little birds have drowned in bathrooms when it didn't need to happen.

> **YOUR RESPONSIBILITY TO YOUR LOVEBIRD:**
>
> **DAILY**
>
> Change the covering on the bottom of the cage. Give your bird fresh food and water in clean dishes.
>
> **WEEKLY**
>
> Clean the cage and perches of old food.

Birdproofing

Eliminating potential problems and maintaining healthful conditions in your home and your lovebird cage will prevent most health problems. Before you buy your bird, take care of as many foreseeable problems as possible.

CORDS AND WIRES

Lovebirds chew constantly and they are not discriminating. Unless you have cleared your home of hazards, your bird could quickly find himself in danger or too sick to revive. Put all cords out of sight, including electrical cords and those leading to your phones and antennas. The squish of the plastic as it is chewed seems to be irresistible to lovebirds. To protect birds and cords, place the cords in ½- to 1-inch-diameter PVC piping. Run this piping around the baseboards in the room from the appliance to the outlet. Out of sight, out of mind.

Always keep an eye out for potential dangers when your bird is out of his cage.

PLANTS

Also remove any poisonous plants. Pet lovebirds do not differentiate between safe and unsafe plants. Among the more common toxic plants are ivy, azaleas, elephant ear, euphorbia, potato sprouts and leaves, creeping Charlie, aloe, philodendron and asparagus fern. Never allow your bird to nibble on flower arrangements.

Some flowering plants that are poisonous include snapdragons, hyacinths, hydrangea, daffodils, chrysanthemums, geraniums, holly, oleander, sweet peas, amaryllis, bluebonnets, calla lilies, crocus, larkspurs, impatiens, jasmine lantana, lilies of the valley, mock oranges, morning glories, narcissus, peonies, pinks, poppies, some rosemary and sage and tulips. This list is by no means complete. If your bird eats something you believe is poisonous, call your vet or the ASPCA hot line for help. The ASPCA hot line number is (800) 548-2423. They will charge you $30 for consultation.

LEAD

Lead is another potential hazard. Do not allow your bird to chew any painted surface. Paint, particularly older paint, often contains lead. Other things contain lead, too, including costume jewelry and the seams between panes in stained glass windows. Old collectible toys may contain lead. Some bird toys may also contain lead. Of particular concern in the past have been the little weighted toys that birds love to knock down and watch bounce back. Curtain weights also may be made of lead. If in doubt, keep it away from your bird.

TEFLON

Another hidden danger is Teflon. At high heat—about 536° Fahrenheit—Teflon and other nonstick coatings on pots and pans emit a gas that can kill your bird. Because birds are far more sensitive to this gas than humans or other animals, you may not know the gas is present until the bird becomes ill or dies. I removed all Teflon-coated pans from my home to prevent an accident. Although I am sure I won't overheat these pans, visitors to my home as well as other family members are not as acutely aware of the problem as I am.

ROOM APPLIANCES

Other hazards include rotating ceiling fans, aquariums without hoods, open toilets, knickknacks and radiant heaters. When your bird is free flying, make sure the room is as safe as possible. Shut all windows and doors; restrain other pets. Try to think ahead of any lurking danger. When I was a teenager, we had two budgies. They flew around the house all day at will, sometimes landing on the screen door to rest. Although we were careful about shooing them away before we opened the door, our dog didn't understand the problem. When she let herself out one day, the two birds flew away.

LEG BANDS

Another common danger is the leg band. Most domestic bred birds will have a leg band to identify the breeder and perhaps the date of birth. I recommend that you ask your vet to take this band off the bird's leg. Keep it in a safe place if you plan to breed or show the bird. I feel strongly about this because of the number of birds that catch this band on hooks, cloth, string or parts of their cages. If left undiscovered, the bird could lose his leg or his life.

All interactions between your bird and other pets should be closely supervised.

OTHER PETS AND CHILDREN

You can have other pets if you have birds, but certain precautions must be taken. Mammal saliva can be toxic to birds if it enters a wound or if the bird ingests it orally. Cats that live with birds should be declawed. Both cats and dogs can be taught to respect and stay away from birds.

89

Some people allow their birds to bite the noses of cats or dogs under controlled conditions to teach the cat or dog to be wary. This works well with cats especially. Of course, the cat or dog must be restrained during the lesson. Still, do not leave a bird and a cat or dog together unattended. I have allowed my large dog to smell my birds, but have impressed upon her with verbal commands that she is to leave the birds alone. She does, but I don't leave them alone together.

It is generally not a good idea to allow lovebirds access to birds of other species, even other lovebird species. Lovebirds are territorial and may injure or kill the other birds, or because lovebirds don't seem to judge their own size correctly, a lovebird may attack a larger bird and become injured or die in the ensuing battle.

Children can also be a danger. They move quickly and are often unaware of how fragile a bird can be. If the bird bites a child, the natural reaction may be fatal to the bird. After children are about 4 or 5 years old, you can teach them how to handle a bird safely.

A Sick Lovebird

If she sits on the bottom of her cage instead of on her perch, she is probably desperately ill. Healthy birds perch as high as they can. Instinctively, birds seem to know that sitting high up helps to keep them away from danger. Well birds sleep balanced on one foot. Sick birds tend to sleep on two feet. Other signs of illness include discharge from a bird's nose or beak or both. If the beak begins to grow at an odd angle or suddenly begins to overgrow and appear to need trimming, your bird may have become ill.

Also look closely for other signs of sickness, such as labored or wheezing breathing and productive sneezing (in which a discharge comes out of the bird's nasal passage). Feather problems can also signal illness. Clubbed, or odd shaped feathers, bald patches on the bird's body, excessive scratching and screaming as the bird yanks out feathers all indicate the need to see a veterinarian.

If your bird appears to be ill, call your veterinarian for an appointment immediately. Don't try to diagnose the illness yourself. Birds are complex animals; it is difficult enough for an experienced avian veterinarian to determine what is wrong and which treatment methods will be most effective.

Proper Use of Medications

Many over-the-counter medications are available in retail stores. Do not use them unless you have been directed to do so by a veterinarian. These preparations could mask the signs of the bird's illness, making it more difficult to diagnose as the bird becomes progressively more ill.

If your avian vet prescribes an antibiotic, be sure to administer it exactly as ordered. This includes using all of the medication. If you stop early, you may give the infection a chance to become immune to the medication. In addition, an over-the-counter drug could kill the beneficial bacteria in your bird's gut, allowing harmful bacteria to grow unchecked. Such a drug might also aggravate the bird's condition, making him sicker than he was before you medicated him.

Administer all medication exactly as your lovebird's veterinarian orders.

Lovebird Health Concerns
PARASITES

Despite what you may read in many other lovebird books, especially those written for European or Australian keepers, parasites in pet lovebirds are uncommon. Never use insecticides in your bird's cage, nest box or on your bird. In North America, where avian veterinarians are available to most people and their birds, I strongly recommend against birdkeepers'

trying to diagnose any health problem—including parasites.

If your bird is thin or losing weight despite a hearty
appetite or if he shows some unusual beak growth
or odd looking scales on his legs, take him to your
vet for an accurate diagnosis. Never install a mite protector in your bird's cage. These are not only ineffec-
tive, they are dangerous to your bird's health.

FIRST AID

Regardless of how careful you are, your creative little
lovebird may require first aid to keep him stable until
you can get him to a qualified veterinarian.

Torn or Bleeding Toenails

Never allow your bird's toenails to overgrow. If they
have become so sharp that they are uncomfortable

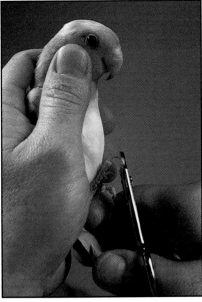

on your finger or shoulder, it's
time to trim them. Allowing a
bird's toenails to overgrow can
be dangerous. Long, sharp toenails can catch on parts of
the cage, in fabric around the
house or on cloth or hemp
perches. If a claw tears, the bird
could bleed to death. In addition, the bird's claw could catch
and panic the bird, causing her
to chew off her leg. Prevention is simple: Keep the bird's
nails trimmed.

Ask your vet to show you how
to do this. Take your own towel
to hold the bird. This ensures
that the towel used has no

*Keeping your
lovebird's nails
trimmed will help
prevent bleeding.*

harmful bacteria. Like doctors' offices, veterinarians'
offices can harbor bacteria and viruses from other
birds' illnesses. When you cut the toenails, keep styptic
powder, cornstarch or flour nearby to press against the
nail if you cut too deeply and bleeding occurs. Apply

pressure until the bleeding stops.

Broken Beak

If your bird breaks off the end of his beak and it begins to bleed, you can stop the bleeding with styptic powder or, my favorites, flour or cornstarch. With your finger, press a pinch of the powder against the wound for a minute or more. Pull your finger away. If blood begins to soak through the powder, put pressure back against the wound until the bleeding stops. Next step? Call the veterinarian.

Blood Feathers

Blood feathers are another source of potential problems. All birds molt, or lose feathers, at least once a year. Although a normal molt will not cause bald patches, you will know your bird is molting because he will lose enough feathers that you will notice. As new feathers grow in, they are supplied with blood. When they finish growing, the blood supply is cut off.

A blood feather is one that is still growing and has a blood supply. The base, or shaft, of the feather looks dark red, whereas other feathers have a clear shaft. If a bird breaks a blood feather, blood will flow freely from the damaged shaft.

To stop the blood flow, pull the blood feather out with a sturdy pair of tweezers. If you cannot do this or are unsure of how to do it, staunch the flow of blood with cornstarch and take the bird to your vet, who will show you how to do it.

If you decide to clip your bird's wings regularly, you must avoid any blood feathers. Cutting one will be especially painful for your bird and will cause it to bleed profusely. Once again you will need to pull the feather. Before I cut wing feathers, I look at them carefully to locate blood feathers; I leave several feathers intact around the blood feather to protect it from the normal wear and tear that will be inflicted by the bird.

Simple Cut or Laceration

A simple cut or laceration may bleed. To stop this, press a clean gauze pad against the wound until the bleeding stops. Do not put an antibiotic cream made for humans on the wound unless instructed to do so by your vet.

Shock

Shock is another condition requiring first aid. This can result from a bird's collision with anything solid, such as a wall, window or mirror. If you suspect shock, wrap the bird loosely in a towel to keep her warm and still for a few minutes. If you and your bird have bonded closely, hold her your chest so she can hear your heart beat. In a minute or two, the bird should recover.

If the effects linger, call your vet. Remember, though, to keep the bird warm while you transport her to the vet's office.

Egg-Binding

Egg-binding can cause significant problems. Your understanding of the condition and knowledge of how to treat it could save your bird's life. Of course, only female birds are afflicted with this problem, but because it is difficult to tell males from females in some lovebird species, you may not be sure of the sex of your bird.

Unmated females can and will lay eggs; usually a healthy lovebird will have no problems laying eggs. An egg-bound female cannot pass her egg. This results not only in the retention of the egg, but the prevention of her passing waste material. Signs of the condition include feather fluffing and sitting on the bottom of the cage looking miserable.

Pick up the bird gently to visually examine her vent area under her tail. If she appears to be swollen, suspect egg-binding. Handle her cautiously; breaking an egg inside a bird can result in disastrous, perhaps fatal, infection. First, wrap her in a towel to keep her warm. Pull the towel apart enough to reveal her vent, under her tail. Carefully apply petroleum jelly around her cloaca and return her to the towel. Call your veterinarian immediately.

Other Animals

Most of us have other animals in addition to birds. If you do, allow your bird out only when you can observe all interaction carefully. If your bird is bitten by a cat or a dog or if the cat or dog has licked or taken your bird in his mouth, take the bird to the vet immediately. The cat or dog saliva is toxic to birds, and requires an antidote without which the bird will die in about forty-eight to seventy-two hours. Each twelve-hour period that passes without treatment decreases the bird's chance of survival. Think of this bite as similar to the reaction some humans have to bee stings.

Broken Bones

Fractures occur rarely, but given the lovebird's active, inquisitive nature, they cannot be ruled out. If your bird breaks a leg or wing, wrap him gently in a towel and take him to your vet, who will know how to splint it. If you are told to bind the bird's wing to his body, use the gauze bandage in your first-aid kit.

Hospital Cage

If your bird has required first aid from you and second aid from your vet, she may also need to be kept in a hospital cage with perches placed low to the floor and food handy. Your vet will be able to advise you, depending on the bird's condition. I keep on hand a small plastic hamster carrier that I use only for one pair of birds. The sides are straight and the lid has openings to allow the free flow of air through the top of the carrier. I put small removable perches in this cage near the bottom with food dishes placed on the wall nearby by suction cups. I cover the floor with plain white paper towels.

The Animal Toxicology Hot Line

If your bird eats something poisonous, you can call this hot line for information on what to do immediately. Have on hand the name of the substance you believe poisoned your bird. If it is a manufactured item, have the product name and the amount the bird ingested.

Although the number is on an 800 line, each call will cost you $30. In some cases, the manufacturer of the product will pay the cost, but don't count on it. Keep this number posted and in your bird's first-aid kit: 1-800-548-2423.

Molting, Feather Plucking and Other Feather Problems

If you find feathers around the house or in the bottom of the cage, how can you tell if your bird is sick or if the loss is due to the natural process of molting? Just as animals lose and replace skin, birds lose and replace feathers. This natural process is called molting. With some birds that are kept in warm homes, this can be a constant process. With others, it will occur only once or twice a year. Factors determining how often the molt will occur can include weather, humidity and number of daylight hours, as well as general nutrition and health.

A bird that is molting may lose what seems to be an alarming number of feathers. Suddenly you will find them everywhere, big and little, down feathers and wing feathers. The amazing thing is that you will not see bald patches on your bird while he molts. Shortly after you begin to see the lost feathers, you will notice small pin-feathers growing on your bird, most noticeably on his head.

Your bird can preen himself to remove the feather casings from feathers on the rest of his body, but he cannot reach those on his head. If he will allow you to, you can gently remove the casing with your fingernails after the blood has receded. If your bird will not allow you to do it, you can cuddle him in a towel after a bath and gently rub his head to remove some casings. In any case, the bird will rub his head on perches, furniture and cage sides and bars to remove the casings.

Feather picking is a condition caused by the bird pulling, or plucking, her own feathers or sometimes a mate's feathers. If it is self-mutilation, the cause should be found. This can range from parasites to low humidity in a heated or air-conditioned house, to low humidity in the climate in which you live, to poor nutrition, to psychological causes.

Once a bird gets in the habit of picking her own feathers, it may be difficult to get her to stop. Once established, the habit is something like fingernail chewing. Those who don't do it don't understand it. Those who do it seem to find it irresistible. If the problem is low humidity, daily baths and/or a cold room humidifier might help. If the cause is poor nutrition, only a better diet will remedy the situation.

If your bird begins to pick her feathers, take her to your vet to rule out all physical causes. If no disease or parasite is the culprit, it's time to analyze the problem. First, look at what has changed. Did you move the cage, add a pet, add guests, hang a new picture on the wall or change her food? Are you feeding the bird less often or at different times than you used to feed her?

If you can, remove causes of stress. If you have ruled out stress as the cause, look at simple boredom. Lovebirds are active, curious, intelligent birds. They need something to keep their minds occupied or they will turn to pulling feathers to pass the time. Lots of toys and plenty of time to play out of the cage with sufficient attention from you should prevent this from starting.

A FIRST-AID KIT

It's easy to put together a kit that will help you take care of your bird if she injures herself. In some cases, such as cuts, broken nails or bleeding blood feathers, you can handle the bird's injury yourself. Keep these supplies in a separate box in a handy place. Use the supplies only on one bird or pair of birds.

A clean towel

Paper towels

Sterile gauze pads

A sterile gauze bandage roll

Masking tape or nonallergenic tape that removes easily

Petroleum jelly

Cornstarch, flour or styptic powder (must be powder)

A notepad and pen to write down doctor's instructions

A small flashlight, such as a pen light

Cotton swabs

Blunt-edged tweezers

Sharp scissors

The phone number of your veterinarian and the Animal Poison Toxicology Hot Line.

Enjoying
Your

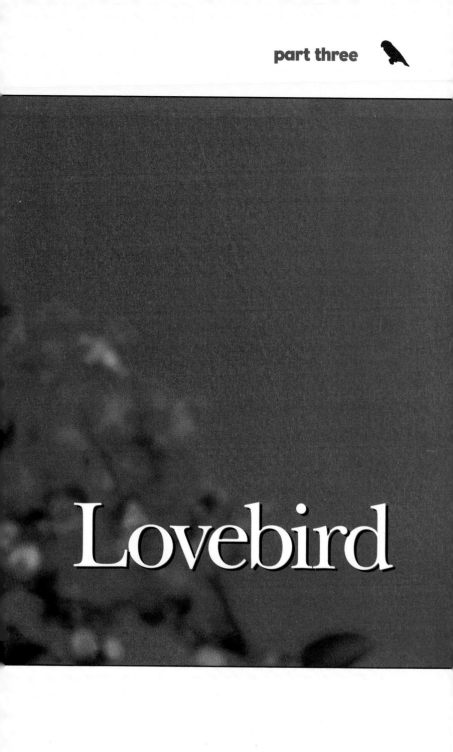

part three

Lovebird

chapter 8

Your **Lovebird's** **Behavior**

Taming and training are all about trust. You may be a bit afraid of your lovebird and her beak, so you will have to learn to trust your bird, as well as your instincts, in order to judge how your bird will react to certain situations. First and foremost, though, you will have to help your bird learn to trust you. Until you get to know and love one another, you and your bird are strangers, and you have all the size and strength on your side.

Imagine yourself in your new bird's position, suddenly living with a total stranger who is hundreds of times your size. If

100

you think of it this way, it will be easier for you to formulate a plan of action that doesn't further frighten and traumatize your bird.

Building Trust

The temptation with a new bird is to bring him home and begin a training session immediately. This can terrify your bird and undermine his potential to trust you. Instead, allow him four to seven days to explore his cage, get used to the daily schedule in your home and observe you and your family in action.

Continue normal activity. Talk to your bird often in a quiet voice, using his name frequently. Put your hands in or on the cage as little as possible, except during cleaning sessions and when offering treats. Parrots regard their cages as their territories. Lovebirds are territorial and will not welcome an invasion of that sort, which can erode their trust of you or your family members.

Before you begin the training session, have your vet clip the bird's wings. Ask that both wings be clipped. If only one wing is clipped, the bird can still fly, but cannot fly straight and is likely to get hurt as he tries to get away from you during the training session. While the vet is trimming the wings, observe carefully so you can carry out this procedure in the future, if necessary. Ask about blood feathers. They have a distinct look and once you have seen them, you can easily recognize and avoid them.

Clipping the wings will make your bird more dependent on you. He will recognize his altered state immediately, and he will be easier to tame. Later, if you wish, you can let the wing feathers grow back so the lovebird can enjoy flying again.

Training Equipment

Before you begin training your bird, assemble the necessary equipment. You should have on hand a wooden dowel-type perch, your bird's playgym or bird stand and some millet and sunflower seeds.

I know trainers who recommend gloves, but birds are afraid of them, and they can only make it more difficult, if not impossible, to convince your bird that your intentions are good. Even birds that have never seen gloves fear them; they have a difficult enough time with bare hands.

Your bird may bite you during the training session, and lovebirds do have a strong bite, but you will buy her confidence more easily if you don't wear gloves. If your bird bites you and will not let go, place you thumb and forefinger on opposite sides of her beak, on the skin where the upper mandible meets the lower mandible. Press gently on this area with your fingers. The bird should release you. If she does not, pry the beak apart with two fingers. Put the bird on her perch and begin again.

A playgym is a great place to start training your lovebirds.

A Special Place to Train

Next, choose a room in which you will work with your bird each day. It should be small and contain few pieces of furniture and no knickknacks. I prefer the bathroom for training because it meets those qualifications. Cover any furniture with drop cloths, cover the windows and mirrors and close any doors. If there is a fireplace, close the flue so the bird cannot fly up the chimney.

If you use the bathroom, close off the bathtub and shower and shut the toilet lid. Remove or hide all electric cords. If you are training in a room without carpet, put a blanket or quilt on the floor to cushion the bird's crash landings. Perhaps the best place to train is inside a stall shower that is large enough for you to sit in.

Another great training spot is a bathtub. If you have a large Jacuzzi-style tub, you can sit in it with your bird. With his wings clipped, the bird cannot fly out of the tub. Lacking this, try using a regular-size tub. In this scenario, you will kneel outside the tub, reaching in to work with your bird. Before you begin work in a shower or tub, cover the bottom with thick towels.

THE TRAINING SESSION

Bring your bird's cage into the training room with a clock, the perch or playgym, a dowel perch and treat seeds. The actual working part of the session should not last more than fifteen minutes to avoid exhausting the bird—and possibly your patience. Work alone, without other people or animals around.

Set the cage on the floor and sit down on the floor several feet away. Talk quietly to the bird, calling him by name and allowing him to get used to his surroundings. When he seems more relaxed, open the

One of the first training lessons is the "Step up."

door to his cage. Gripping one end of the dowel perch, slide it slowly into the cage as you continue to talk to your bird. Put the perch under the curve of the bird's abdomen, just above his legs. Push up and in (gently but firmly); this will put your bird a bit off balance, forcing him to step up and onto the perch. As you are doing this, say, "Step up." Pull the bird and perch out of the cage to begin the session.

If this method does not work, open the cage door and allow the bird to come out on his own. You can tempt him with treats, then sit quietly and wait for him to come out of his cage. Then push the perch up under his abdomen to encourage him to step on. Never grab your bird or use a net. Grabbing will scare your bird and set back the training schedule. Netting a bird can result in panic and injury.

Once the bird is on the dowel, move it toward you slowly—at about the level of your face. Talk to him gently and in a reassuring manner. If he flies away, don't chase him with the dowel. Let him sit on the floor until he calms down. Move toward him, still sitting, not standing. Attempt to get him to step up on the dowel again. Put him on the playgym. Sit nearby, talking to him in a pleasant voice, calling him by name.

Stepping onto your hand is a big accomplishment for a lovebird.

When the bird seems more composed, encourage him to stand on the dowel again. End the session fifteen minutes after actual work on the dowel begins. During the next session, repeat your actions. After the bird is used to getting on the dowel, it's time to teach him to step onto your hand. To do this, squeeze all fingers together, as you hold your hand in a horizontal position, thumb tucked tight to the hand. As the bird sits on the dowel or on his playgym, push your hand up under his abdomen, putting the bird off balance, so he will step onto your hand. This is a huge step for a bird.

Talk to him as you work and offer some millet or a sunflower seed, if you wish. A little peanut butter on your finger or hand might tempt even the wariest bird. If that's what tempted your lovebird to step onto your hand, give him time to eat some before you continue the session. Always move slowly as you work with your bird. End each session about fifteen minutes after it began. If your bird was hand-fed and is still young, he should tame in a short period of time. It's difficult to predict exactly how long it will take. That can depend on your personality, your bird's personality and his experience with other humans, whether he was hand-fed or parent-raised and how young he is.

Incorporate your lovebird's natural talents when teaching tricks.

GIVING AFFECTION

When your bird will step confidently onto your hand, then you can begin to train her to accept petting and kissing and then to cuddle. This must all be done in the same unhurried manner as the early training. If you want to pet your bird, begin by touching her abdomen with one finger. She may bite, but after many sessions, your bird can learn to not only accept this touch, but to welcome it.

Petting her abdomen can be followed by petting her head. This may be more difficult. Many birds fear having a hand over their backs. If she was hand-fed, though, the breeder gently cupped her head and back in a hand, and she will be used to this position. After your bird accepts petting, you can begin the sometimes slow process of teaching her to cuddle.

If you are working with a young bird that has black on her beak, the training sessions will yield the desired results much sooner than if the bird is older or was parent-raised. Such birds are still trainable; it will simply take more patience and a longer time to accomplish the task.

After your bird is finger-tame, you can work with others on training sessions. Children may be the most difficult because they talk loudly and move quickly.

105

Tricks and Treats

Have you ever watched a bird show and wondered how the trainer taught the bird those tricks? Successful trainers watch their birds carefully to learn about their natural behaviors. They then plan tricks that are based on these performances.

Hey—look at the neat trick I learned!

If your bird enjoys calling out, you can teach him to answer when you call his name. This training must be done in increments. Call the bird's name. If he makes a noise—any noise—praise him and give him a treat. After he has made this step, call again and reward only a larger step, like a louder noise, until you get to the call stage you are looking for.

Other natural actions to incorporate into tricks are flying and climbing. Don't expect to teach your bird to talk, though. In only a few rare recorded instances have lovebirds learned to talk. These birds have so much to recommend them that the ability to talk is not high on my list of what I require of them. No one should ever buy a bird to teach him to talk; expecting something of him that he may not be able to give is a surefire way to disappoint yourself and mistreat a bird. Even among species known to talk, some birds will never utter a word.

THE WELL-TRAINED LOVEBIRD

I know of a Peach-faced Lovebird that had been parent-raised and then bought by a busy couple, both of whom were attorneys. While they loved their little bird, they were easily rebuffed and did not work with him to tame him. When he was several years old, the couple took an extended vacation and asked a friend to take care of their bird. The friend was not only self-employed, she was calm, patient and at home with him all day every day. Within a month, he came out of his cage for free flight each day. When she called, he flew to her and nestled in her hand for a nap.

Traveling with Your Bird

When you travel with your bird in the car, always carry her in a closed container. It's tempting to let her sit on your shoulder or the back of your car seat; however, if you are involved in a traffic accident or if you absentmindedly open a window, your bird could be lost. Many styles of bird carriers are on the market, some from mail-order catalogs advertised in bird magazines. I have several kinds of travel cages for my birds. One is made of acrylic. Because I ordered it directly from the manufacturer, I asked that three sides and the top be made of smoke-colored acrylic, to help make the bird feel more secure. Another great travel cage is made of wire and folds flat to about the size of a briefcase.

The ideal travel container can be used in a car, a plane or a train. It should have at least one perch and food and water dishes. If you are traveling a great distance, you may find it more convenient to offer fruit in place of water, which spills easily. Attach the carrier to the seat with a seat belt, and keep the bird inside her carrier while you are traveling.

Avoid overheating or cooling the bird. This includes keeping the bird away from direct sunlight and heating and air-conditioning vents. If you plan to travel by plane, make reservations ahead so you can take your bird inside the plane's cabin. Often, only one pet is allowed inside each part of the cabin: economy, business and first class.

When we moved this last time, one bird rode in the car in her car carrier, and I transferred her to the travel cage when we got to the motel each night. All of my birds' travel cages and car carriers have sturdy locks and a label with my name, phone number and address. This label is attached in case I am in an accident and have lost consciousness. Anyone who found the birds would know who I am and that the birds belong to me.

chapter 9

Having Fun
with Your
Lovebird

In order to understand your pet, it is important to consider how lovebirds socialize in the wild. This will help you understand their social and emotional needs.

Fearless Lovebirds

Their powerful personalities belie their small size—tiny lovebirds seem fearless. Most are undaunted by larger, louder, more powerful animals of any species.

As you might not expect of such fearless birds, they are sociable with each other and with humans. It is important to understand, however, that they can also be quite aggressive with one another and with other pets, including birds that are much larger. Lovebirds have been known to kill others of their own species as well as larger or smaller birds. Peach-faced Lovebirds are reputed to be the most aggressive of the nine lovebird species.

Lovebirds are active, seeming sometimes to be constantly on the move, whether flying, climbing or walking on whatever surface is available to them, with a cocky confidence you will surely find amusing. Fischer's Lovebirds are clownishly acrobatic and require a lot of space, either an aviary or a large cage and a great deal of freedom. Masked Lovebirds may be shy compared to Peach-faced Lovebirds, but their ways are endearing.

The most frequent source of complaint about lovebirds is the raucous screech some make. Of these, the Peach-faced is perhaps the noisiest, with a loud, harsh screech. This call can be set off by something obvious to all, like a loud, frightening noise, or by something so subtle only the birds are aware of it. Noise is relative, though, and although they make a harsh call, the noise level is nowhere near that of a barking dog, crying child, screaming cat or screaming larger parrot. Before you buy a lovebird, visit a store or a breeder and stay long enough to hear them vocalize.

Lovebirds have the capacity to be aggressive towards other birds.

Talking Ability

Some people get interested in parrots solely because they can talk. Reality is that only some can talk. No one can guarantee that any bird, even one of a species known for talking, will talk. Still, each bird has her own interests and personality—much like humans or any other animal.

If you are interested only in a bird that will learn to talk, a lovebird is not the species for you. It is a rare lovebird indeed that talks. I have read of three or four—after extensive research on talking birds—but have never heard one talk and do not know anyone who has.

Frankly, the likelihood of a lovebird learning to talk is about slim to none. Frequently, a species' ability to learn human language is based on the kind and extent of its species' verbal communication among flock members in the wild. This said, there are many other reasons to choose a lovebird as your pet. Watching a lovebird explore his environment and enjoy life is one of the most incomparable experiences anyone can have. To be a special part of this gregarious parrot's life is a privilege that can't be matched by much else.

Lovebirds don't talk—but they have more personality than words can express.

I have kept birds since I was 13 years old. Some have talked, but the majority have not. Most of my favorites never uttered a word. They were full of life and curiosity, though. They wanted my love and attention and they repaid me in full by keeping me company and entertaining me. They also opened my eyes to the world of animals around me and the interesting behaviors exhibited by animals everywhere. This is a fantastic gift.

Playtime!

Now that you are all set up and have gotten acquainted with your lovebird, it's time to do what you intended all along: Have fun! There is hardly any better companion to have fun with than a lovebird. I still remember the first hand-fed lovebirds I saw. A breeder had about twenty of them together in a big basket. It was early spring, and the little chicks looked like a basket of rollicking little hand-dyed eggs. The memory still brings a smile to my face.

One reason lovebirds are so much fun is their boundless zest for life and the energy level that backs it up. Lovebirds are, in many ways, like small children. They play hard, and they attack everything they do with great enthusiasm. If you have a playgym for your bird, you can introduce new toys there, leaving much of the cage for flying. Your bird will enjoy a great variety of toys, but some will become special favorites. As you come to know your bird, you will begin to recognize which toys will be a hit and which will have no appeal for your bird.

> ### TRAINING TIPS
>
> Start slowly and with simple tasks.
>
> Keep training sessions short and positive.
>
> Teach tasks that come naturally to your bird.
>
> Give your bird lots of praise and occasional food rewards.

Natural behaviors help determine some toys all lovebird owners should start with. Lovebirds adore climbing. Capitalize on that with ropes that hang from the ceiling, or smaller ropes hung from the playgym or attached tightrope style from the top of the bird's cage to the playgym. You may already have a wooden swing in the cage, but hanging one from your ceiling or a tall, nontoxic plant will add to your bird's fun, giving him a resting spot when he is flying freely.

CLIMBING TOYS

Rig up a series of ladders for your bird to climb. Several new styles on the market allow you to build elaborate ladder systems, tinker toy style. Hang welded chains from perches on the playgym or cage. Be sure the links are all welded so there is no chance of your bird getting any part of his foot stuck in the small space that is sometimes found between the two sides of a chain link.

After your bird gets used to his toys and you have watched him play for awhile, you can begin to see which activities he particularly enjoys and repeats. Using these, you can teach your lovebird tricks that will entertain both of you. Tricks are best taught in small increments. If your bird likes to climb ladders, for instance, you can begin by rewarding him with a tiny bit of a favorite treat each time he climbs a ladder. Add a word with the action, such as "Up." Say the word each time the bird successfully climbs the ladder. Then give the bird the treat. After a time, you can only give the treat when the bird goes up the ladder after you have said the word. When this is instilled, you can add other elements.

Hanging toys are ideal for lovebirds since they are enthusiastic climbers.

BELLS

Bells are another great lovebird favorite, and you will be delighted to see your bird learn to ring a bell. Choose small bells made for lovebird-size birds. Avoid the round "jingle bell" types; the slits in their sides make them dangerous to little beaks that might easily become trapped there. To teach your bird to ring the bell on command, wait until she rings the bell on her own. Give her a treat and say a command, such as "Ring." Repeat this method. Later, say the command when the bird is near the bell but has not rung it. If the bird moves closer to the bell, give the treat. The next step will be to say the command and offer the treat only when the bird has responded by ringing the bell.

CUDDLING

Some lovebirds, especially those that were hand-fed, like to cuddle in their owners' hands. A lovebird that enjoys closeness might choose to sleep in his owner's hands or a pocket. This, too, could be incorporated into a trick. Once again, start small. If you want the bird to go into your pocket, begin by feeding him small portions of a favorite food whenever he comes near your pocket. You can tempt him toward your pocket with the food. When he is comfortable with that behavior and reward system, put a treat in your pocket. Let the bird see you put the treat in your pocket. As curious as most lovebirds are, it won't be long before he will want to see what's in there. Offer him a treat merely for looking the first few times. As he becomes used to looking in the pocket, withhold the treat, except for the one in your pocket. In time, he will go into the pocket to get the treat.

Each bird is an individual with his own personality. You will soon know what he will do and what he won't even try. Some birds will be too active to want to take part in anything as passive as climbing into a pocket. Those are the ones that will love learning to climb a ladder and ring a bell, or fly from swing to swing on cue. Other tricks you might try include climbing down a ladder or a rope on cue, putting things in a cup or toy, and chirping for a treat. Practicing while teaching the trick and showing off the results will give both you and your bird hours of fun.

Fun Games

Another game with a purpose involves a towel. It is invaluable to have trained a pet bird to allow herself to be wrapped in a towel. Once this has been taught, you will find it easy to clip her toenails, to examine her for potential injuries or to let your vet examine her without causing her undue fright.

Instinctively, birds do not like to be contained or trapped. Towels can be terribly frightening to them. To get yours used to a towel, you can begin by playing games with the bird. I prefer to use towels that match my bird's ground color, thinking that they are perhaps more comfortable with those colors. For lovebirds, a green similar to their body color is the best. If you do

*You can teach
your lovebird to
enjoy being held
in a towel
through trick
training.*

not have a towel this color, choose one that is tan or white. Avoid bright reds and oranges or combinations of those colors with black. These are colors that often mean danger in the wild.

Show the bird the towel in several play sessions. Let your bird climb all over the towel. When the moment seems right, loosely wrap the towel around your bird. Let her climb out at will. As in trick training, take your time. Speed will only panic your bird and delay the training. When your bird allows you to wrap the towel around her body, pet her head and chest gently so she will learn to associate good feelings with the towel. Play peek-a-boo and other little games with the towel. This way, the towel will signify fun to your bird and to you. When it's time to restrain your bird for a more serious purpose, she will not panic.

TOGETHERNESS

While you find your bird endlessly fascinating, he will also find you pretty interesting. He will enjoy climbing in and under your hair, in and out of pockets, inside your shirt and up your shirt sleeves. All of this is good fun for both of you. Birds are flock animals and, as such, they like to do things in a group, from playing to eating. You may find that your bird eats best if he can see you at mealtimes. Offer him a plate on top of his cage containing those foods that are safe for him to eat.

Birds will often try a greater variety of food if they can see other "flock members" eating it, too. This is a good time to feed cooked foods, because you will remember to remove them from the bird's cage when your meal is over. In my house, the birds rule supreme. My menu planning has a great deal to do with things my birds like to eat. Favorites are scrambled eggs, chicken cooked any way possible, beef and any vegetables. The birds especially relish chicken bones from well-cooked chicken. If the bones seem too tough for them to crack open and eat the marrow, I crack them with a nutcracker.

KEEPING IN SHAPE

If you have left your bird's wings intact or have let them grow again after the taming process, you should schedule regular free-flight sessions everyday. This will help keep your bird from gaining excess weight and will give her a great deal of happiness. To make you happy, too, remove all plants or other items that are either toxic or irreplaceable.

Although it may seem like a wonderful idea, do not take your lovebird outside. A puff of wind could blow your tiny friend away or a predatory bird might pluck your bird from your shoulder and carry her off.

Questions from New Owners

About the time I began writing this book, several friends bought their first lovebirds. When you bring home a new pet, one who is totally dependent on you for all of his needs, you will probably have many questions and concerns. Noting that my friends all asked mostly the same questions, despite the differences in age, gender and places they lived, I decided to include the most asked questions here, hoping to answer some of your questions, too. Each of these pet owners had owned his or her bird(s) from a few days to a few months when I recorded our conversations.

Q: I brought my bird home about two days ago, and she shakes whenever I come near. Is she cold or afraid of me? What can I do?

A: Although I suspect that your bird is still unaccustomed to you and the rest of her new surroundings, we need to look at the whole picture. If the temperature inside the house is about the same as that of the pet store or the breeding facility, she should be warm enough. Check to make sure your bird is not under a vent, either for air-conditioning or heating. If there is a ceiling vent in the room, tape the ends of slender strips of paper to it. Watch the strips when the heating or air-conditioning system is on; they will show you which direction the air blows. If your bird is in a direct pathway, move the cage. Also make sure your bird is not in front of a window or doorway.

If temperature is not the problem, then make sure your bird feels secure. Remember that she is in a new environment. Try to put yourself in her place. Back the cage against an interior wall, preferably in a corner to give her security on two sides. Those are two sides that she knows no one can suddenly appear from. An interior wall is one that is not part of the outside perimeter of your home. If your home is not well insulated, the temperature variation through walls that are affected by outside conditions could be great. If you can, provide a nontoxic plant barrier, such as a schefflera, on one side to give the bird some privacy. Leave the front of the cage barrier free so the bird can see you and your family.

Beyond that, simply take your time approaching and gaining the trust of your new little pet. Talk to her softly and reassuringly. Use her name often. Offer treats. In a few months, you will wonder what happened to that shy bird you once knew.

Q: My bird flew into a glass window and was stunned. She was pretty quiet for about thirty minutes. I didn't know what to do. Will that injure her permanently? What can I do to prevent this?

A: Flying into glass windows, doors and mirrors presents a danger to birds that are allowed free flight. Before you let your birds out to fly, first make sure all windows are shut and doors are shut and locked. Until you are sure of your bird's flying habits, cover any mirrors she might crash into. If you have some sort of window covering, put it in place. Later, you can uncover mirrors bit by bit, as your bird gets used to their presence. If you notice that your bird still tends to fly into a mirror, keep it covered when the bird is out or move it from the room.

When a bird flies into a hard surface, such as a wall or window, pick her up gently and hold her in a clean towel to keep her warm. Check the bird carefully but gently for any broken bones or shattered blood feathers. If you notice any such injury or if the bird doesn't return to her normal, active state quickly, call your avian veterinarian.

Q: My bird and I just had our first training session, and I noticed his feet are hot. Does this mean he has a fever? How do I know if he has a fever?

A: Never try to judge the state of a bird's health based on your own. A bird has a higher metabolism and heart rate than a human, and his normal temperature is higher as well. Some of the signs of illness include decreased appetite, diarrhea, discolored droppings, inactivity, sleeping on two feet, fluffed feathers and sitting on the bottom of the cage. Those signs will tell you to talk to your avian veterinarian, who will know how to take and evaluate your bird's temperature.

> **HANDICAPPED LOVEBIRDS**
>
> Handicapped birds can make wonderful pets. If the bird is missing a leg or cannot fly, you can buy hamster cages with ramps that can accommodate a damaged bird. Ladders, sleeping platforms, wide perches and other accessories make it possible to house one of these little birds well. Sometimes parents or other birds in an aviary attack babies; this may be one of those birds. She could use a good home. I have one bird that is missing a toe. On the day we clip toenails, we are glad!

Q: I know my bird needs clean water to drink, but she keeps getting in her water dish to bathe. How can I keep her out of it?

A: Most lovebird species enjoy bathing and they will decide when and where they will take this bath. You need to supply not only clean drinking water but also a separate dish for bathing each day. If you are already doing so, but your bird bathes in both, consider using a water bottle for drinking and a dish for bathing. Remember, though, that this bottle must be exchanged with a clean one once a day. Keep two or three on hand, and wash them in the dishwasher to remove all bacteria.

Q: How many toys are too many? I go to buy one or two toys and find myself walking out with many more. The cage is looking kind of crowded.

A: Rotate new toys in and older toys out periodically. Remember, your lovebird needs room to move around. I would recommend no more than three at a time.

Q: My bird bit me. Does that mean that he doesn't like me anymore?

A: Birds bite for all kinds of reasons. If you and your bird had a good relationship previously, more than likely your bird was simply expressing one of many emotions, possibly surprise, anger, fear or jealousy. Your bird might also have been hungry, over tired or out of sorts. Feeling the same way, you might be cross with your friends.

On the other hand, your bird could be feeling unwell. Watch him closely to see if he shows any other signs of illness. One other possibility is that your bird is trying to control you. If you decide this is the case after eliminating all other possibilities, you can alter your bird's perception of who is in charge with a few changes. Clip your bird's wings. This will make him feel dependent on you.

Whenever you allow your bird out of his cage, put your finger under his abdomen, push up and give the command, "Step up." Do not allow your bird to ride on your head or sit above your eye level, which will make him feel physically superior to you. Birds are not pack animals like dogs, and they are more intelligent than most cats and dogs. Out-thinking them can be great fun.

Q: I want my lovebird to cuddle, but he just won't do it. He acts like he will bite me if I try to pick him up and cuddle him. What can I do to change him?

A: Each bird has his or her own personality. Some like to cuddle and some do not. You can try to gradually coax your bird to sit on your hand, then in the palm of your hand. Later, if this is successful, you can try gradually cupping your fingers around your bird.

The key is to do all of this slowly. If at any time your bird looks panicked, back off. Your bird may never be a cuddler. Respect that. Look for some other way to enjoy each others' company, such as sharing peanuts, playing with shredded paper or learning tricks.

Q: My friend has a lovebird, too. We want our birds to be friends. How should we introduce them?

Q: Should I take my bird to bird club meetings? I see other people there with their birds and I want to show off mine, too.

Q: My bird throws tantrums when I leave the house. I'm tempted to take him with me and just let him ride on my shoulder, like he does at home.

A: These three questions require a similar answer. It's best to limit your bird's contact with other birds and with other bird owners. The more contact your bird has with birds that live outside your home, the greater his chances of becoming ill. You want to show off your bird, and your bird hates it when you leave home, but resist the temptation.

Don't worry if your lovebird doesn't want to cuddle. Like people, lovebirds have unique ways of showing affection.

Q: I bought two lovebirds because I was told that they would only be happy as a pair. Now they pay lots of attention to each other, but not to me. I wanted one or two birds that would pay a lot of attention to me. What can I do now?

A: The truth is that lovebirds are best kept alone if you want them to interact with you. Now that you have two, you could consider giving one to a friend, but the birds will most certainly mourn during a separation period. If you do this, you will have to be certain to give your remaining bird enough attention to make up for the loss of his friend.

Most important, this level of attention must be maintained every day—not just the first few days or weeks after you have separated the birds. If you can make this level of commitment, you will surely succeed. I would separate a pair of birds that get along well only if they have been together a short time—a few weeks. If they are lifelong buddies of many months or years, they may not be able to make the adjustment, leaving everyone unhappy with the new arrangement.

Q: I bought two lovebirds and they fight all the time. Is this how they are supposed to behave? What can I do?

A: You may have two birds of different species, or two birds that just don't like each other. I would separate these birds. Put them in two cages, perhaps across the room. Let them out of their cages at different times.

Q: I have read that birds are easier to care for than cats and dogs. I want a lovebird, but I travel a lot on an irregular schedule. Can I just leave the bird alone in my apartment for several days?

A: Birds are social animals and need daily interaction. Hire a pet sitter or ask a friend

A pair of lovebirds are more likely to bond to each other than their owner.

to take your bird home while you're gone. Some avian veterinarians board birds, and staff members keep a close watch on their state of health. Ask bird club or birdkeeping friends for recommendations.

Q: How do I know if I am overfeeding my bird? Can lovebirds become obese?

A: Lovebirds are so active, they will rarely have problems with gaining weight if they are getting enough exercise. Allow your bird free-flight time every day, and plenty of toys she can climb on and swing from. In addition to fruits and vegetables every day, also provide cooked low-fat food. With exercise and a proper diet, your bird's weight shouldn't become a problem. If you think your bird is overweight, discuss the problem with your avian veterinarian.

After a few months, you will become comfortable with your bird and his needs and habits. Simple observation will help you understand most of the questions you once had about your bird. You will also know exactly when to get professional help from your avian vet. Buying a lovebird as a companion pet may be one of the best things you will ever do. In exchange for the room, board and affection you provide, your bird will give you unconditional love, which will certainly improve the quality, and perhaps the length, of your life.

part four

Beyond the • Basics

Resources

Books

Alderton, David. *You and Your Pet Bird.* New York: Alfred A. Knopf, 1994.

Bedford, Duke of. *Parrots and Parrot-like Birds.* New Jersey: TFH Publications, Inc., 1969.

Brokmann, Jörgen and Werner Lantermann. *The World of Lovebirds.* New Jersey: TFH Publications, Inc., 1990.

Doane, Bonnie. *My Parrot My Friend: An Owner's Guide to Parrot Behavior.* New York: Howell Book House, 1994.

Doane, Bonnie. *The Parrot in Health and Illness.* New York: Howell Book House, 1991.

Forshaw, Joseph M. *Parrots of the World.* New Jersey: TFH Publications, Inc. By arrangement with Doubleday and Co., Inc., 1977.

Freud, Arthur. *All About Parrots.* New York: Howell Book House, 1980.

Freud, Arthur. *The Complete Parrot.* New York: Howell Book House, 1995.

Gallerstein, Gary A., DVM. *The Complete Bird Owner's Handbook.* New York: Howell Book House, 1994.

Lowell, Michele. *Your Pet Bird*. New York: Henry Holt
and Company, 1994.

Ritchie, Branson W., DVM PhD, Greg J. Harrison, DVM
and Linda R. Harrison. *Avain Medicine: Principles and Application*. Wingers Publishing, Inc., 1989.

Magazines

Bird Talk. Monthly magazine devoted to pet bird ownership. Subscription information: P.O. Box 57347, Boulder, CO 80322-7347.

Bird Breeder. Bimonthly magazine dedicated to the concerns of bird breeders who raise and sell pet birds. Subscription information: P.O. Box 420235, Palm Coast, FL 32142-0235.

Birds USA. Annual magazine aimed at first-time owners. Look for it in your local bookstore or pet store.

Caged Bird Hobbyist. This magazine for pet bird owners is published seven times a year. Subscription information: 5400 NW 84 Ave., Miami, FL 33166-3333.

Online Resources

Bird-specific sites have been cropping up regularly on the Internet. The sites offer pet bird owners the opportunity to share stories about their pets and trade helpful hints about bird care.

If you belong to an online service, look for the pet site (it's sometimes included in more general topics, such as "Hobbies and Interests," or more specifically "Pets"). If you have Internet access, ask your Web Browser software to search for "lovebirds," "parrots" or "pet birds."

American Animal Hospital Association
http://www.healthypet.com

Association of Avian Veterinarians
AAVCTRLOFC@aol.com

American Veterinary Medical Association
http://www.avma.org/care4pets/

Veterinary Information

Association of Avian Veterinarians
P.O. Box 811720
Boca Raton, FL 33481
(407) 393-8901

Write to this organization for a recommendation of an avian veterinarian in your area.

Bird Clubs

African Lovebird Society
P.O. Box 142
San Marcos, CA 92079-0142

African Parrot Society
P.O. Box 204
Clarinda, IA 51632-2731

American Federation of Aviculture
P.O. Box 56218
Phoenix, AZ 85079-6218

Australian Aviculture
52 Harris Rd.
Elliminyt, Victoria 3249
Australia

Publishes Australian Birdkeeper, *a bimonthly magazine devoted to aviculture.*

Avian Information and Management
P.O. Box 369
Felton, CA 95018-0359

Avian Information and Management can help you find a bird club in your area.

Avicultural Society of America
P.O. Box 5516
Riverside, CA 92517-5517

Publishes monthly bulletin detailing society's activities.

Bird Clubs of America
P.O. Box 2005
Yorktown, VA 23692

National Cage Bird Show Club, Inc.
25 Janss Rd.
Thousand Oaks, CA 91360

National Parrot Association
8 N. Hoffman Lane
Hauppage, NY 11788

Society of Parrot Breeders and Exhibitors
P.O. Box 369
Groton, MA 01450

Parrot Conservation Organizations

United States World Parrot Trust
P.O. Box 341141
Memphis, TN 38184

Other Organizations

National Animal Poison Control Center Hot Line
(800) 548-2423

Parrot Rehabilitation Society
P.O. Box 6202213
San Diego, CA 92612-0213

The Parrot Rehabilitation Society rescues and rehabilitates abused and neglected parrots.